ORIGAMI+
KIRIGAMI
for the Home

ORIGAMI+ KIRIGAMI
for the Home

Paper Art Decorations, Gift Wrapping
and Handmade Cards

WEI YOU

HERBERT PRESS
LONDON · OXFORD · NEW YORK · NEW DELHI · SYDNEY

HERBERT PRESS
Bloomsbury Publishing Plc
50 Bedford Square, London, WC1B 3DP, UK
29 Earlsfort Terrace, Dublin 2, Ireland

BLOOMSBURY, HERBERT PRESS and the Herbert Press logo are trademarks of
Bloomsbury Publishing Plc

First published in Great Britain in 2022

A catalogue record for this book is available from the British Library
Library of Congress Cataloguing-in-Publication data has been applied for

ISBN: 978-1-78994-082-4; eBook: 978-1-78994-081-7

2 4 6 8 10 9 7 5 3 1

Designed by Lorraine Inglis Design
Printed and bound in China by C&C Offset Printing Ltd

To find out more about our authors and books visit www.bloomsbury.com and sign up for
our newsletters

Scan for origami
video demos!

CONTENTS

INTRODUCTION

Origami (折紙) – taken from *ori* (meaning 'folding') and *gami* (meaning 'paper') – is the Japanese art of paper folding that transforms simple flat sheets of paper into beautiful, intricate sculptures.

Kirigami (切り紙) – which combines *kiri* (meaning 'cutting') and *gami* (meaning 'paper') – has a simple difference in that the paper is cut as well as folded to create equally elaborate three-dimensional designs. Kirigami is a folk art in many places around the world and the patterns often represent the culture behind them, mostly being used as festival decorations. Modern kirigami is often combined with origami to create ornate three-dimensional forms.

Many traditional origami ideas stem from day-to-day life and Japanese culture, from something as simple as teabags, which were made using origami techniques to preserve the flavour of teas from China, to the most well-known origami form, the crane, which is recognised as a symbol of good fortune and longevity. A poem by Ihara Saikaku, which dates back to 1680, depicts origami butterflies being used in traditional Shinto weddings to represent the bride and groom.

From these long-established origins, we step into modern origami. The turning point was the launch of the Yoshizawa–Randlett system in the early nineteenth century – a universal diagramming system used to describe the folds used in origami structures. This system enticed more mathematicians into new computational folding techniques such as corrugation, pleating and tessellation, which were widely introduced in fashion, furniture and engineering design.

The focus of this book is to create beautiful, decorative origami and kirigami pieces that can be made by anyone, regardless of experience. Inside the book, you will find a wealth of ideas taken from traditional origami, from table decorations and tiles to gift wrap and garlands. Easy-to-follow instructions, photographs and clear diagrams will guide you step by step through easy-to-intermediate designs made from simple geometric forms. Some of the finished objects may look complex at first glance, but once you give them a try you will soon understand the idea of the concept behind them and discover they are not as difficult as they first appear!

A couple of new folding styles are included, such as pleating and tessellation, but don't be intimidated – the pieces in this book do not require you to be a professional artist or craftsperson! Only the basic techniques are introduced, making each project suitable for beginners, as well as helping those with some origami experience to build on and develop their skills to create truly impressive makes.

Both origami and kirigami are fantastic hobbies that allow us to focus on mindfulness, enhancing our ability to be aware of what is happening in the moment. By simply engaging with paper and focusing on the folds, touch and texture, we can distract our ever-busy minds and gain an essence of calm, as well as releasing our creativity and enhancing our hand-eye coordination.

Where to start? We begin by going back to basics and looking at selecting paper, with an introduction to paper types. This explores how the weight and finish of your paper can affect the finished result of your origami and kirigami creations, enabling you to choose the right paper for every project to gain the best results. We then look at some basic folds which are useful to master to enable you to become an origami pro!

Origami and Kirigami for the Home will take you through a variety of gorgeous projects, including table decorations and wall art to decorate your home, parties and events as well as unique ideas for presents, cards and gift wrap that are guaranteed to wow the recipient. Throughout the book, you will also find many ideas for alternate colour combinations that change the look of your design to suit the occasion.

Paper is more than just a blank page to write on. A gift that is made out of paper carries a message and a wish from the heart. It will last forever, ageing beautifully as time goes by.

PAPER
AND TOOLS

Paper

Paper is a great material to use for making decorations. People often think that it is fragile and won't last long, but it is stronger than you would think. There are many different types of paper to choose from, each with different properties, so it is worth considering your paper choice for each project carefully to achieve the best results.

Origami Paper

Standard origami paper is around 60 gsm, single-sided and comes in a multitude of colours. It is fine, easy to crease and suitable for most origami projects, such as the Beautiful Blossom on page 56. The most popular size is 15 x 15 cm.

Tant Paper

Tant paper is around 80 gsm and is used for several projects in this book, such as the Tant Crane on page 90. Tant paper is made for folding and is suitable for both simple and complex origami forms. It is gentle

Origami paper

to fold with but feels rough to the touch, and you can see the grains throughout. Tant paper is also famous for its colour and shades, from dark bright colours to soft pastel tones. For beginners, a pack of 15 x 15 cm multicoloured tant paper is recommended.

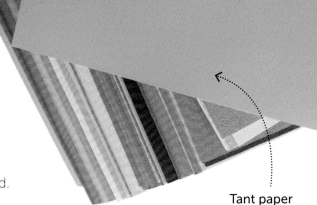

Tant paper

Copy Paper

Coloured copy paper is a cost-effective option for kirigami and a good choice for feathered cranes and paper flowers, as well as the Spooky Bat (page 144) and Halloween Garland (page 147). You can buy mixed colour packs of 80–115 gsm paper, which are available in over twenty shades.

Newspaper and Magazines

Newspaper and magazines are very good, readily available recycled materials which can be used for both gift wrapping and kirigami. The Exotic Crane on page 88 is crafted from magazine paper.

Handmade Paper

A selection of handmade papers are introduced in this book. You may find that, due to the making process, the weight of handmade paper is not even; some parts of the paper get really thin and the barks can make the paper difficult to fold. But the natural dyed colour and texture give a unique finish, making this paper suitable for folding.

Mulberry Paper

Mulberry paper, at around 30 gsm, is one of the most popular options, used on the Eight-petal Flower on page 40. It is very fine, soft and silky to the touch, with visible fibres.

Chinese Xuan Paper

The Chinese xuan paper is used for the Pretty Pentagon Flower (see page 20). This paper is very fine and smooth, like silk, and was traditionally made for calligraphy and painting. The paper comes in a natural white and slightly off-white colour. It is soft but not as fragile as mulberry paper.

Chinese xuan paper

Washi

There are many other handmade papers available that allow you to have beautiful designs with an array of textures on your finished pieces. Washi (和紙), a Japanese paper processed by hand and made in the traditional manner from local fibres, is used in many of the projects in this book. The Hinode Crane (see page 32) uses Yuzen washi, while the Square Flowers (see page 66) are made with Torinoko washi. The mix of long fibres in making washi makes it one of the best papers for gift wrapping; a more durable alternative to standard wrapping paper.

Chiyogami

Chiyogami (千代紙) is an exquisite hand screen-printed paper from Japan, commonly used in papercrafts. It is a decorative washi with detailed screen-printed patterns. Its beautiful vibrant patterns are inspired by traditional motifs and nature throughout the seasons. It adds character to simple origami pieces, such as the Colourful Doves on page 52. The paper weight is around 80 gsm, which makes it easy to fold, and it has a soft feel that is similar to cotton.

Tools

You will only need a few basic tools and materials to get started with your origami and kirigami designs.

Washi paper

Glue

Clear glue or tacky glue are used in most of the projects in this book. They are suitable on most surfaces and dry clear.

Double-sided Tape

Double-sided tape is useful in gift wrapping to achieve the neatest edges.

Wooden Skewers and Pegs

Wooden skewers and pegs are useful tools for holding and fixing paper, for example while glue is drying.

Hanging Strips and Hooks

Damage-free hanging strips and hooks are used on hanging frames and ceiling decorations. They hold strongly and can be removed easily.

Florist Wire

This is useful for making stems for paper flowers.

Washi Tape

Originating from Japan, washi tape is a low-tack, decorative, durable masking tape that can be used to add pattern and colour to projects.

HOW TO READ ORIGAMI INSTRUCTIONS AND SYMBOLS

Folding Symbols

These basic origami symbols, lines and arrows are the 'language' of origami, used in the diagrams throughout the book. These symbols, or origami expressions, are based upon those developed by Akira Yoshizawa and modern internationally recognised conventions. In order to be able to successfully fold from diagrams, you will need to familiarise yourself with them.

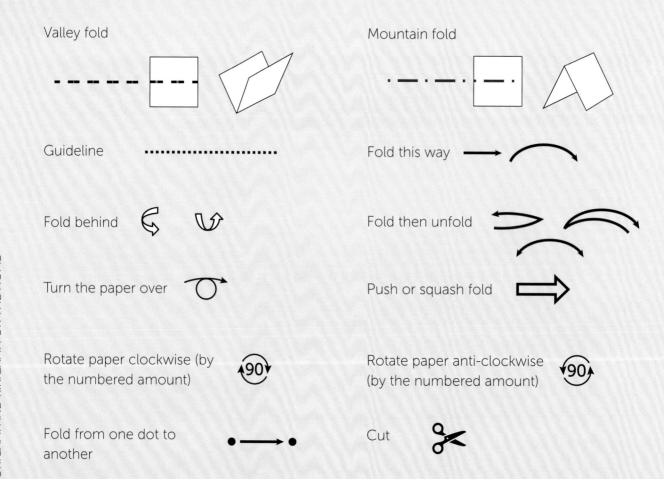

Valley fold

Mountain fold

Guideline

Fold this way

Fold behind

Fold then unfold

Turn the paper over

Push or squash fold

Rotate paper clockwise (by the numbered amount)

Rotate paper anti-clockwise (by the numbered amount)

Fold from one dot to another

Cut

Basic Folds

These traditional basic folds are important to learn and master as they often feature in origami model creation. As they form the foundation of many projects, it helps to practise them again and again to get the best results for your finished makes.

Squash Fold

1 Hold the paper at a diagonal. Fold the paper in half from corner to corner.

2 Valley fold in half along the centre line and unfold. Then bring the top corner down to the bottom point and unfold.

3 Open the top layer of your paper at the central vertical crease line and bring the flap's corner to the bottom corner.

4 Finished!

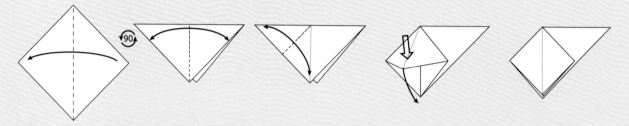

Inside Reverse Fold

1 Fold the paper in half diagonally.

2 Valley fold the top tip at an angle towards the open side, then unfold.

3 Mountain fold along the crease line, then open the folded tip and bring the paper down.

4 Finished!

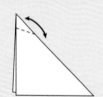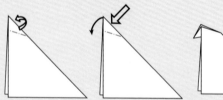

Outside Reverse Fold

1 Fold the paper in half diagonally.

2 Fold the top tip at an angle towards the centre fold, then unfold.

3 Open the paper and then, following the crease lines, bring the tip back over the paper and fold the paper back in half.

4 Finished!

Waterbomb Base

1 Fold diagonally both ways and unfold.

2 Turn the paper over. Fold in half both ways, then unfold.

3 Turn the paper over. Bring the mountain fold lines inwards to the bottom edge of the centre line.

4 This is how it will look mid-fold!

5 Finished!

Scan for a tutorial!

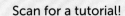

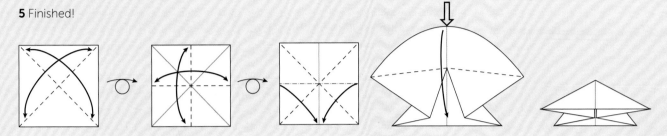

Rabbit Ear Fold

1 Hold the paper at a diagonal. Fold from corner to corner, then unfold.

2 Bring the left hand side down to the centre horizontal line, and unfold. Repeat on the right-hand side, making sure that your crease lines cross the vertical line.

3 Follow the crease lines and fold the sides in and down towards the centre line.

4 Bring the standing-up corner over to the side, and collapse the paper completely down to the centre line.

5 Finished!

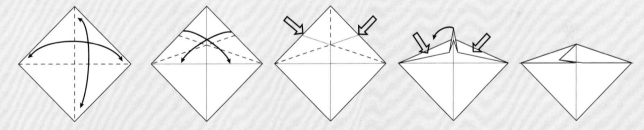

Pleat Fold

1 Make a valley fold on your paper, in the upper half, making sure it is a straight line. Leaving a small gap, make a mountain fold below.

2 Bring the lower half of the paper up, following your creases, to make a zigzag.

3 It will look like the pleat of a skirt or accordion, and can be continued with more parallel folds to create further pleats.

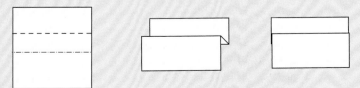

HOW TO READ ORIGAMI INSTRUCTIONS AND SYMBOLS

17

TABLE DECORATIONS

Introduction

Making table decorations is a fun introduction to decorative origami and a beautiful craft project to have a go at. Centrepieces, place cards and napkin rings can all be made from paper, bringing a unique and personal touch to your table decoration that will impress your guests at a dinner party or any special celebration meal.

A few different types of paper are used in this chapter to show how the beautiful textures reflect onto the origami pieces. Yuzen washi gives beauty and character to the place cards (see pages 32–39), while Chinese xuan paper adds softness to the Pretty Pentagon Flower (see page 20) and mulberry paper brings a touch of delicacy to the Eight-petal Flower (see page 40). You can choose different colours to mark the occasion: try reds, golds and greens for your Christmas dinner table, oranges and yellows for an Easter lunch, or bright shades and fun patterns for a birthday party.

This chapter starts with beautiful centrepieces, including a graceful swan and a stunning pentagon flower design, which can both be made in bulk to create an eye-catching table focal point. The contemporary Fabulous Flower Vase (see page 23) can be filled with an array of assorted paper flowers for a unique personalised display.

We then move on to place card holders, with two classic cranes, suitable for beginners, and a more detailed geometric design that will add a contemporary personal touch to your seating plan. Finally, a napkin is just not complete without a napkin ring, and the fun flower and flamingo designs will lift this accessory to another level. Just don't get so carried away dressing the table that you run out of time to prepare the food!

CENTREPIECES
PRETTY PENTAGON FLOWER

Make a bunch of these gorgeous paper flowers and arrange them
in a glass vase for a floral arrangement with a difference!

MATERIALS

- 1 sheet of 15 x 15 cm Chinese xuan paper (I used multiple sizes, including 10 x 10 cm and 20 x 20 cm)
- Scissors
- Skewer (optional)

DIFFICULTY ✳✳✳

INSTRUCTIONS

1 Fold the paper in half from bottom to top.

2 Fold the bottom right corner up in half, and unfold.

3 Bring the top right corner down in half and pinch, crossing the diagonal line.

4 Bring the bottom left corner up to the crosspoint on the folded line.

5 Fold the corner of the flap back on itself.

6 Bring the edge (highlighted in blue) to the fold you made in step 5.

7 Bring the right-hand flap behind the left side.

8 Cut the paper, keeping in line with the front flap.

9 Open up the triangle.

10 Expand to a folded semicircle shape.

11 Open it up part way (11a), bring the red dots together and the bottom point, then turn your paper to the side (11c).

12 Fold the top flap up.

13 Bring the top corner down towards the single flap. There will be three top and two bottom flaps.

14 Turn over. Bring the bottom corner of the top flap up to the centre line but fold only halfway along, then unfold.

15 Bring the lower side of the triangle up to the horizontal line (following the red dots), then unfold. You will have a line that meets the half line from step 14.

16 Repeat steps 14–15 on the top half. Make sure your lines cross over on the horizontal line!

17 Fold the tip of the triangle to where your lines cross over in the centre.

18 Unfold everything.

19 Mountain fold along the central pentagon's creases then follow the valley folds on the surrounding paper.

20 Turn your paper slightly to the side, follow the valley crease as marked and flatten the fold.

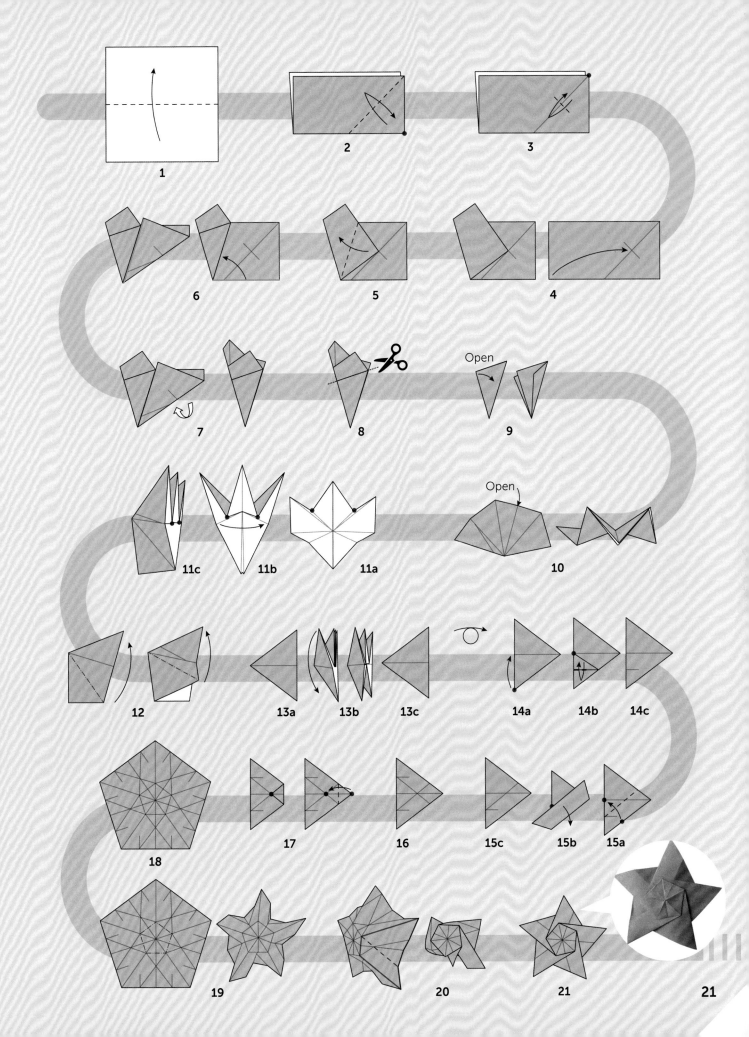

1

2

3

6

5

4

7

8

Open

9

11c 11b 11a

Open

10

12

13a 13b 13c

14a 14b 14c

18

17

16

15c 15b 15a

19

20

21

21

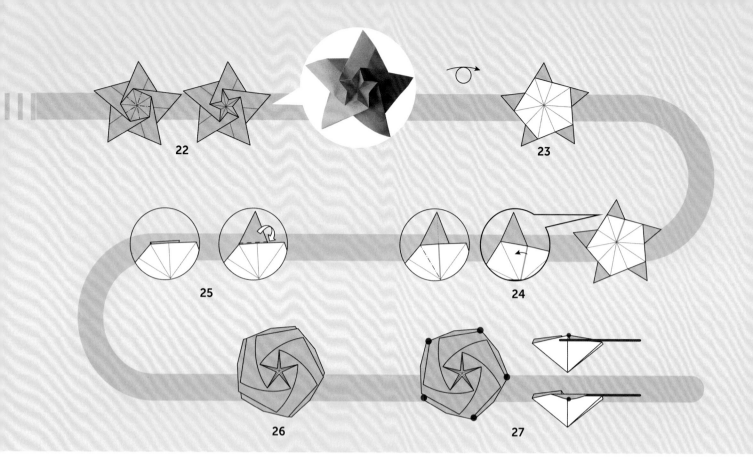

21 Repeat step 20 on all the corners. Make each valley fold strong and then move your hand around the shape and press down once you have them all secure.

22 Make mountain creases on the side folds of the pentagon to make a star shape.

23 Turn the paper over.

24 Mountain fold one segment in half so that the outer edge (highlighted in blue) is in line with the tip of the point above.

25 Fold the pointed triangle behind the top layer of the star. Repeat for all points. You should see the paper curve towards the inner star and create a flower.

26 Your Pretty Pentagon flower is now finished!

27 Optional: curve the pointed corners down with a skewer.

Scan for a tutorial!

FABULOUS FLOWER VASE

This contemporary vase design can hold any paper flowers of your choosing, here I've chosen a bouquet of Pretty Pentagon Flowers (page 20). Use thin wire to form their stems and hold them in place for a dazzling display.

MATERIALS

- 1 sheet of 25 x 25 cm Chiyogami paper
- Pencil
- Ruler
- Scissors
- Clear glue
- Skewer (optional)

DIFFICULTY

INSTRUCTIONS

1 Fold the paper in half from bottom to top.

2 Fold in half again from right to left.

3 Bring the top-left side over to the right side.

4 Bring the back piece to the right side, keeping at the back.

5 Folding at the corner of the folded side, bring the bottom right corner up to just below the top left edge.

6 Turn the paper over. Extend the flap out to the right side.

7 Bring the bottom edge up to the left side.

8 Your paper will look like this!

9 Using a ruler, draw a line from the left-hand corner of the flap. It should line up with the corner flap on the other side of the paper.

10 Cut along your drawn line. You should have a triangle left.

11 Unfold the triangle – it will now make a hexagon. Fold up the bottom edge to the centre line, then unfold.

12 Repeat step 11 to each edge.

13 Fold the bottom edge up to the centre line.

14 Following the crease lines, open up the bottom right corner and bring the right-hand side over the bottom flap to the centre line.

15 Repeat step 14 on the right edge.

16 Repeat step 14 on the top edge.

17 Repeat step 14 on the left edge.

18 Open up the left-hand flap. Open the bottom and top edges out and bring them over, keeping the base hexagon shape. Make a rabbit ear fold and bring the sticking-up flap over to the right.

19 Fold the bottom flap over to the left – each top triangle will now be a flap in the hexagon.

20 Fold the top flap's right corner down to centre point.

21 Repeat step 20 on each of the remaining flaps, then unfold each of these.

22 Open the top flap and fold the back bottom corner (lower red dot) up to the upper dot, in line with the flap's centre line.

23 On the next flap clockwise, fold the point up from the centre so it is in line with the corner of the previous flap, and its edge matches up with the far fold line.

24 Repeat step 23 on the remaining flaps.

25 Fold the top flap back to the centre point.

26 Mountain fold the tip of this flap and tuck it under the paper. Use glue to fix this to the upper underside if it doesn't hold the crease well.

27 Repeat step 26 to all the remaining flaps.

28 Turn slightly. Following the mountain fold edge lines, gently push out the sides to raise the folded triangle.

29 Repeat step 28 on each of the remaining triangles, until it is all raised and looking more like a vase.

30 Turn the vase 90 degrees anticlockwise, and gently mountain fold each of the triangle corners to round the shape.

31 Your Fabulous Flower Vase is now finished!

32 Optional: use a skewer to curl the pointed edges inwards.

Scan for a tutorial!

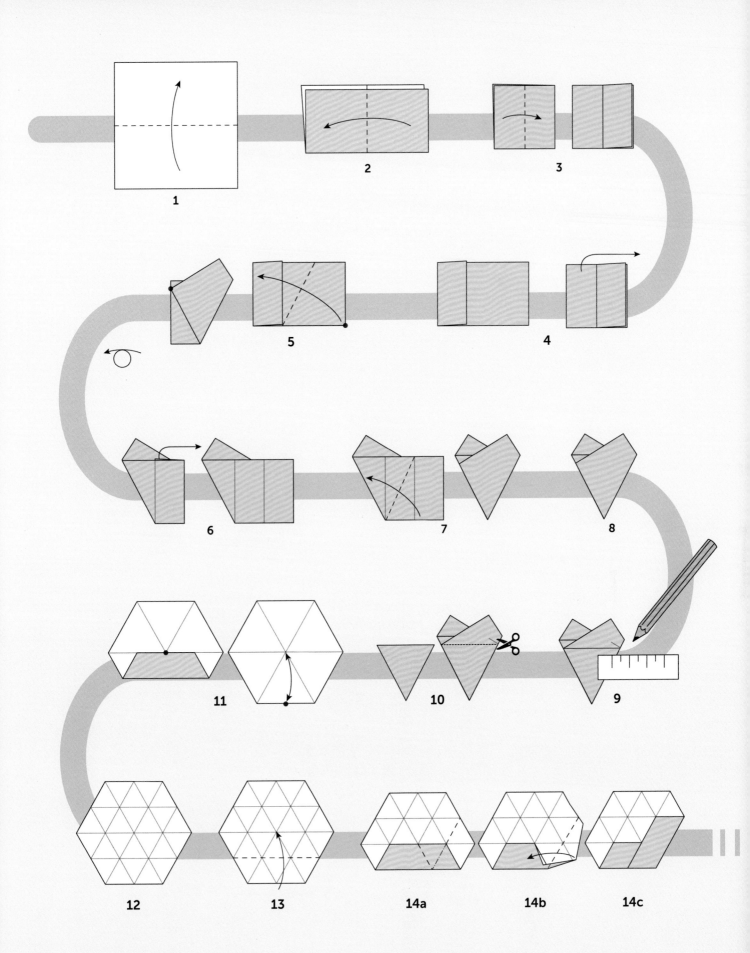

1

2

3

4

5

6

7

8

9

10

11

12

13

14a

14b

14c

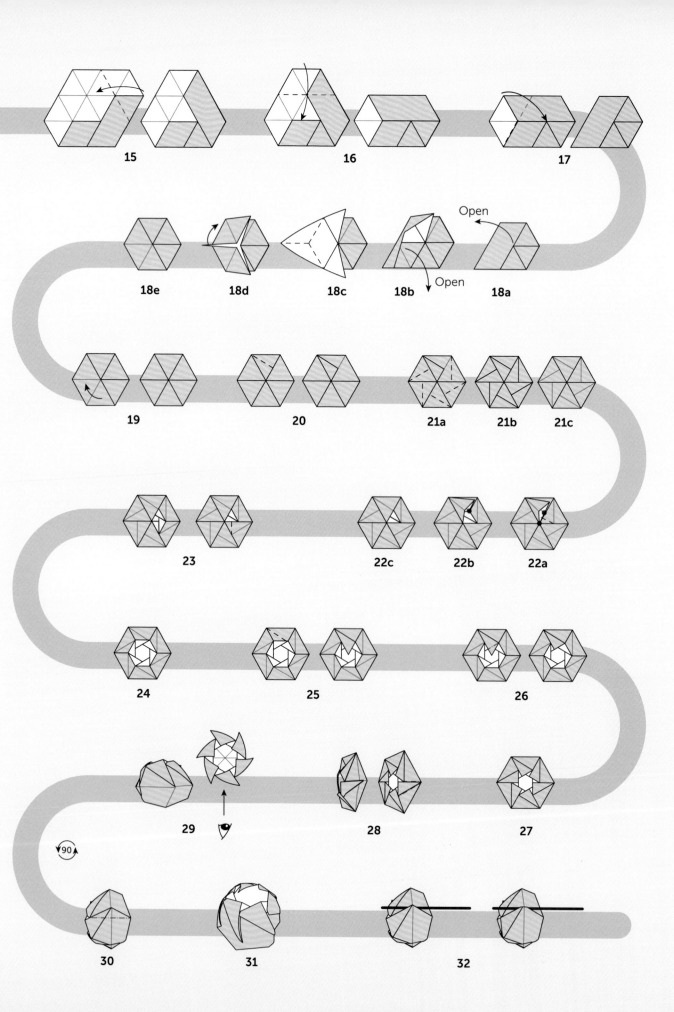

15

16

17

18e 18d 18c 18b 18a

Open

Open

19 20 21a 21b 21c

23 22c 22b 22a

24 25 26

29 28 27

90

30 31 32

MAJESTIC SWAN

This striking swan design will add a touch
of instant elegance to any dinner party.

MATERIALS

- 2 sheets of paper in the same size.
  15 x 15 cm makes a name-card-sized swan;
  use 35 x 35 cm or larger paper for a centrepiece.

DIFFICULTY ✳✳✳✳✳

INSTRUCTIONS

1 Fold in half diagonally and unfold.

2 Fold the left side to the centre crease. Repeat on the right-hand side.

3 Bring the top point down (red dots) and pinch fold from one black dot to the other, then unfold.

4 Bring the left side over to the right.

5 Fold the top of the triangle down and unfold to step 4.

6 Bring the two sides to the centre line, folding from the tip straight to the crease line, then unfold.

7 Make a small crease horizontally from one cross point to another, and one above the triangle point, then find the middle point between these. Valley fold from the middle point to the lower corners.

8 Turn 45 degrees anticlockwise. Follow the existing valley creases (in dark blue), then valley fold along the yellow lines. Fold at a slight angle from the edge of the yellow shape to create red valley folds.

9 Mountain fold the body part. The fold starts from the end point of the green valley folds. Then press the model flat; a new bottom line is formed.

10 Follow the crease line (this is the yellow line from step 8), and bring the upper neck up to the main body.

11 Fold the tip of the neck down at an angle then unfold.

12 Open the face's tip up and mountain fold away from the body.

13 Fold the face's tip down at a slight angle. Unfold.

14 Open up and inside reverse fold down at the crease line.

15 Open the folded tip up, and inside reverse fold the very tip at an angle.

16 Tuck the corner of the top flap behind, then repeat on the other side.

17 Valley fold and bring the whole tail over. Unfold and open apart.

18 Bring the tail tip down following the existing mountain fold creases.

19 Your swan will look like this! Open up the back.

20 Hold your paper to the light to see a diamond shape behind the paper. Find the centre of the diamond shape (blue dot).

21 Make a mountain fold from the centre point to the edge of the paper, bringing the tail up.

22 Fold up the two flaps under the swan, then unfold.

23 Open the base, then tuck in the flaps at the creases.

24 Looking from above, fold and unfold the tail corner at an angle.

25 Make an inside reverse fold along the creases you just made.

26 The swan's body is now complete!

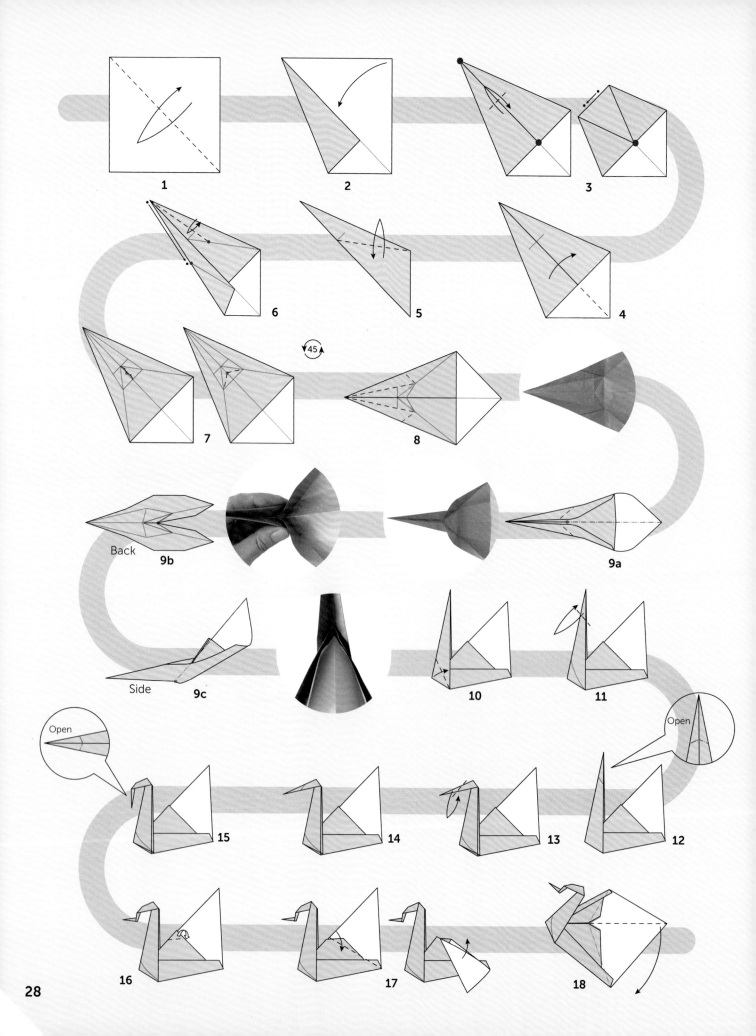

1

2

3

6

5

4

45

7

8

9a

Back
9b

Side
9c

10

11

Open

15

14

13

12

Open

16

17

18

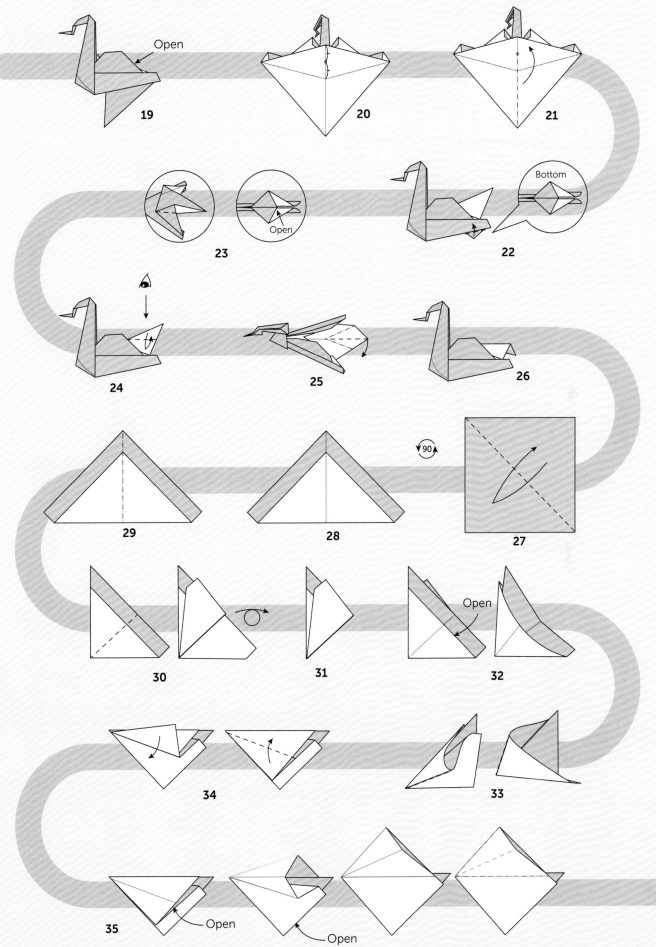

Open

19

20

21

23

Bottom

22

24

25

26

29

28

↺90

27

30

31

Open

32

34

Open

33

35

Open

Open

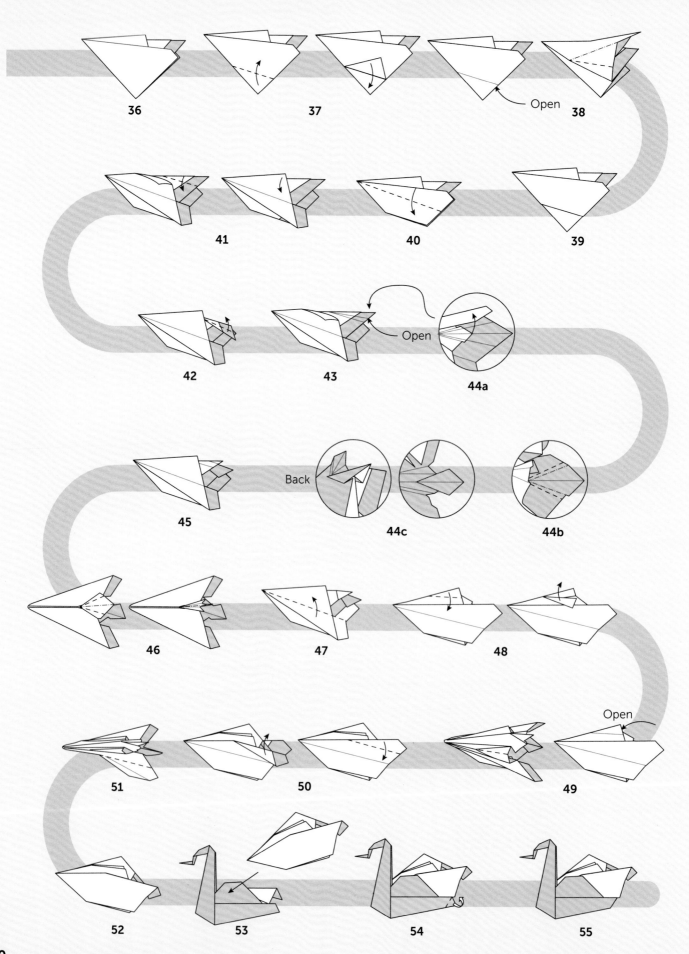

36

37

38

Open

41

40

39

42

43

44a

Open

45

44c

Back

44b

46

47

48

51

50

49

Open

52

53

54

55

27 Using your second sheet of paper for the feathers, fold diagonally and unfold.

28 Rotate 90 degrees anticlockwise and fold in half, leaving a gap of approximately 1 cm on the paper behind.

29 Mountain fold in half.

30 Valley fold the the top flap up in half, leaving a small triangle visible at the top.

31 Turn the paper over and repeat step 30 on the other side.

32 Unfold steps 30 and 31 and open up the outer flap.

33 Bring the paper on each side inwards at the crease line, then tuck in by folding the outer flap on itself.

34 Fold the top flap up and overlap the top line. Then unfold.

35 Open up the top flap and bring down over the centre, following the existing creases and paying attention to the valley/mountain folds. Yellow – valley; green – mountain; blue – valley; purple – mountain.

36 Your paper will look like this!

37 Fold and unfold the corner. This part is the bottom of the wings so there's no strict angle on the fold.

38 Open the folded corner and tuck it in.

39 Repeat steps 37–38 on the other side.

40 Bring the upper flap down.

41 Fold down the side flaps to add layers to the feathers. No strict rules on the angles, but fold the centre tip down in half.

42 Fold the tip up in half.

43 Unfold steps 41–42.

44 Follow the crease lines and raise the tail feathers up.

45 Your paper will look like this!

46 Open the feathers and follow steps 44–45 on the top flap.

47 Bring the lower flap up.

48 Fold over the tip and unfold.

49 Open the folded corner and tuck it in.

50 Fold the lower flap then open and tuck it in.

51 Fold the back flap then tuck it in. Repeat steps 47–51 on the other side.

52 The swan feathers are now complete!

53 Place the feather paper on the swan's back to assemble.

54 Fold the bottom corner behind to secure the feathers. Repeat on the other side.

55 Your Majestic Swan is now finished!

Scan for a tutorial!

PLACE CARD HOLDERS

HINODE CRANE

Hinode means 'sunrise', and the crane is a traditional symbol of happiness and eternal youth. Combining the two creates a place card holder that will fill your guests' hearts with hope and optimism.

MATERIALS

- 1 sheet of 15 x 15 cm Yuzen washi paper
- Clear glue
- Pencil

DIFFICULTY ✳✳✳

INSTRUCTIONS

1 Fold across both diagonals and unfold.

2 Flip over. Fold in half horizontally and vertically, then unfold.

3 Turn over. Follow the mountain creases to form a square base. The bottom point will be open.

4 Bring the top, left and right corners of the top layer to the centre line and unfold.

5 Lift up the top layer and follow the existing creases to bring the sides to the middle.

6 Flatten the sides. A new diamond shape is formed.

7 On the top layer, bring the right-hand side over to the left.

8 Bring the left-hand back layer over to the right then open up the right-hand side fully.

9 Fold the bottom flap up and repeat on the other side.

10 Bring the top corner down to the bottom edge.

11 Fold the whole top of the flap down to the bottom edge, then unfold. Repeat on the other side.

12 Pull out the folded flap to open, keeping the last section on the body.

13 Valley fold the next crease line and bring the paper back to the body.

14 Valley fold the paper down to the bottom edge. Repeat on the other side.

15 Hold the front section and open the layers of the tail. Crease on both sides.

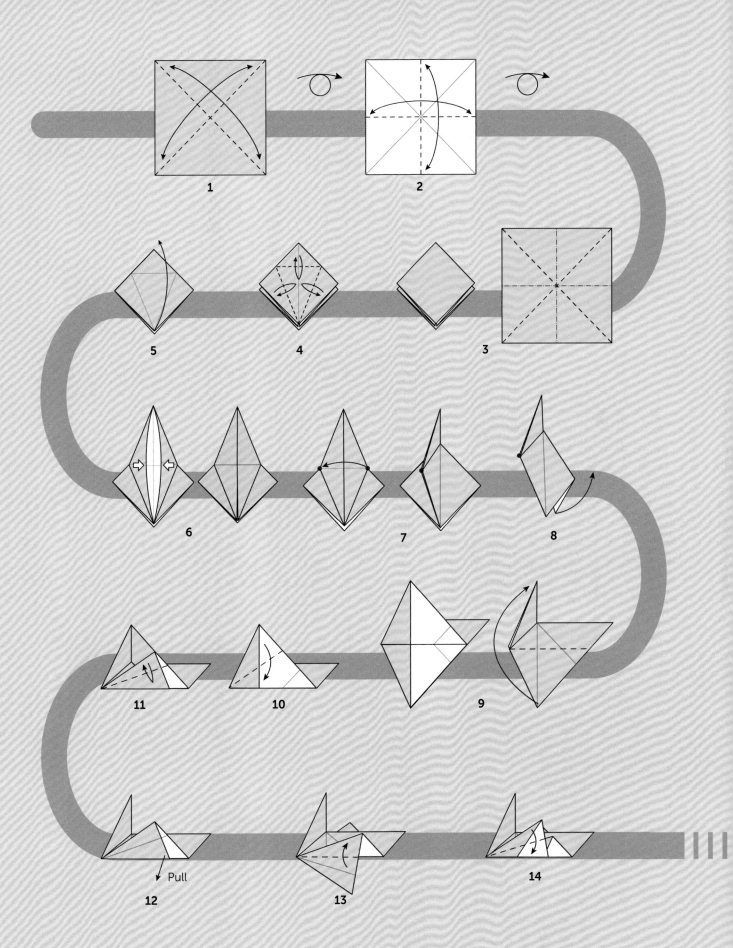

1

2

3

4

5

6

7

8

9

10

11

Pull

12

13

14

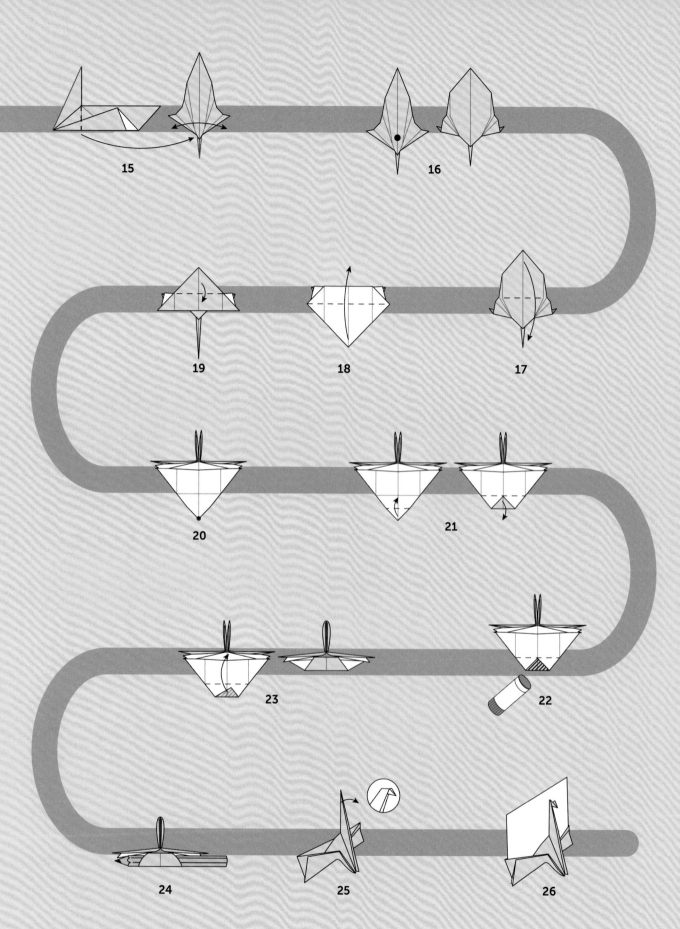

15

16

19

18

17

20

21

23

22

24

25

26

16 Press the central section down to open the paper out fully.

17 Fold the back of the tail to the tip of the face.

18 Fold the tail back, creasing in line with the edge of the wing.

19 Fold the tip of the tail down, creasing in line with the back edge of the wing.

20 Unfold steps 18–19.

21 Fold the tip of the tail of the crane to the next crease line, then unfold.

22 Glue the folded tail.

23 Insert the tail into the pocket on the back of the body. Stick in place.

24 Fix the glue and shape the bottom part with the help of a pencil.

25 Turn the paper so it is upright. Inside reverse fold on the pointed tip to make the crane's head.

26 Your Hinode Crane place card holder is complete! Insert a card as shown.

Scan for a tutorial!

HAKOBU CRANE

Hakobu means 'carrying', and, to me, this elegant crane place card holder brings to mind a carriage bearing a name or wish.

MATERIALS

- 1 sheet of 15 x 15 cm Yuzen washi paper

DIFFICULTY ✲✲✲

INSTRUCTIONS

1 Fold across both diagonals and unfold.

2 Flip over. Fold in half horizontally and vertically, then unfold.

3 Turn over. Follow the mountain creases to form a square base. The bottom point will be open.

4 Bring the top, left and right corners of the top layer to the centre line and unfold.

5 Lift up the top layer.

6 Follow the existing creases to bring the sides to the middle. A new diamond shape is formed. Turn over and repeat.

7 Fold one side up to the middle line and repeat on the back.

8 Bring the folded top-left layer over to the right side.

9 Fold the bottom flap up, then bring the left layer over to the right side.

10 Inside reverse fold on the top flap to make the crane's head.

11 Fold the wing down to the left on the bottom edge, and unfold.

12 Fold the wing down to the right on the bottom edge, and unfold.

13 Follow the existing creases to make a rabbit ear fold.

14 Bring the wing over the left side.

15 Repeat steps 12–15 on the other side.

16 Open up the lower tail.

17 Bring the tail up past the head.

18 Fold the tail down so it lies flat with the rest of the body.

19 Open up the wing to the left side.

20 Mountain fold and tuck in the edge of the wing.

21 Fold the wing back and repeat on the other side.

22 Your Hakobu Crane place card holder is finished!

Scan for a tutorial!

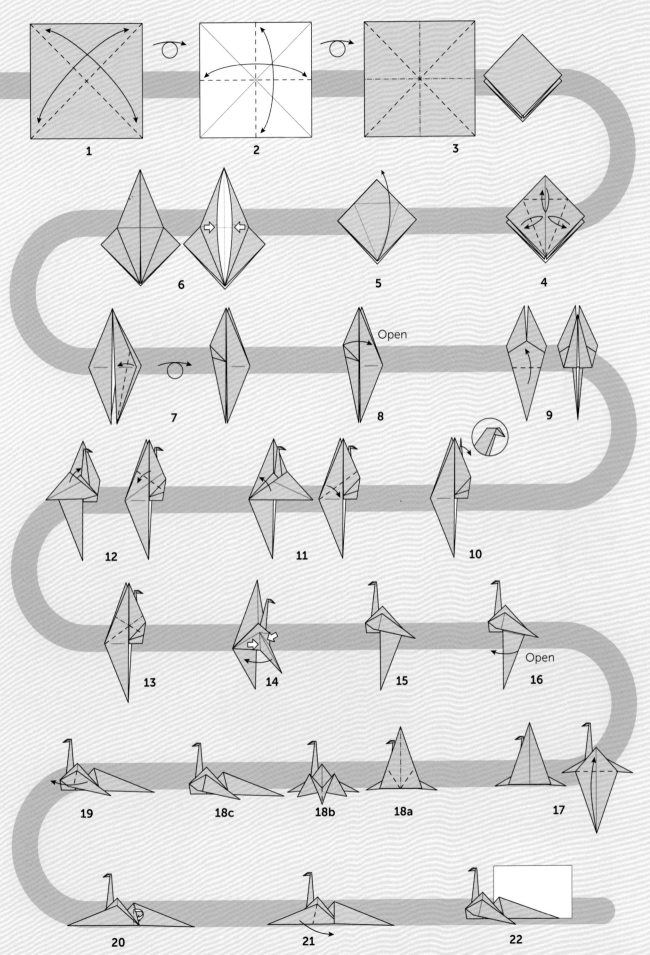

1

2

3

6

5

4

7

8

Open

9

12

11

10

13

14

15

16 Open

19

18c

18b

18a

17

20

21

22

GEOMETRIC BASE

These angular place card holders will instantly add
a contemporary twist to your table decorations.

MATERIALS

- 1 sheet of 15 x 15 cm paper. (For the deep blue place
  card holder I used tant paper; for the pink floral and
  yellow floral variations I used Yuzen washi paper.
  You could also use printed origami paper)
- Clear glue
- Pegs

DIFFICULTY ★★★★

INSTRUCTIONS

1 Fold across both diagonals and unfold.

2 Flip over. Fold in half horizontally and vertically, then unfold.

3 Turn over. Follow the mountain creases to form a square base. The bottom point will be open.

4 Fold each corner point towards the centre line, and unfold.

5 Lift up the top layer and follow the existing creases to bring the sides to the middle.

6 A new diamond shape is formed. Repeat on the other side.

7 Looking underneath, pull the top flaps out and open the middle section until you have a square with triangles on both sides.

8 It will look like this! Neaten the sides of the middle square.

9 Turn the paper over. Open the upper flap up.

10 Flatten the lower flap up.

11 Bring the tip down towards the bottom edge.

12 Bring the edges towards the centre. An overlap is fine here.

13 Turn 90 degrees clockwise. Repeat steps 10–12 on the next flap. Apply the same folds (steps 10–12) on the remaining corners.

14 Open the flaps you have just folded. Looking from the side, your base will now be three dimensional.

15 Apply glue to the shaded area and stick to the flap next to it. Make sure to leave the top corner of each flap un-glued so that it can hold a place card.

16 Repeat step 15 to the remaining three sides. Use a peg to hold the glued area while it dries.

17 Your Geometric Base place card holder is complete!

Scan for a tutorial!

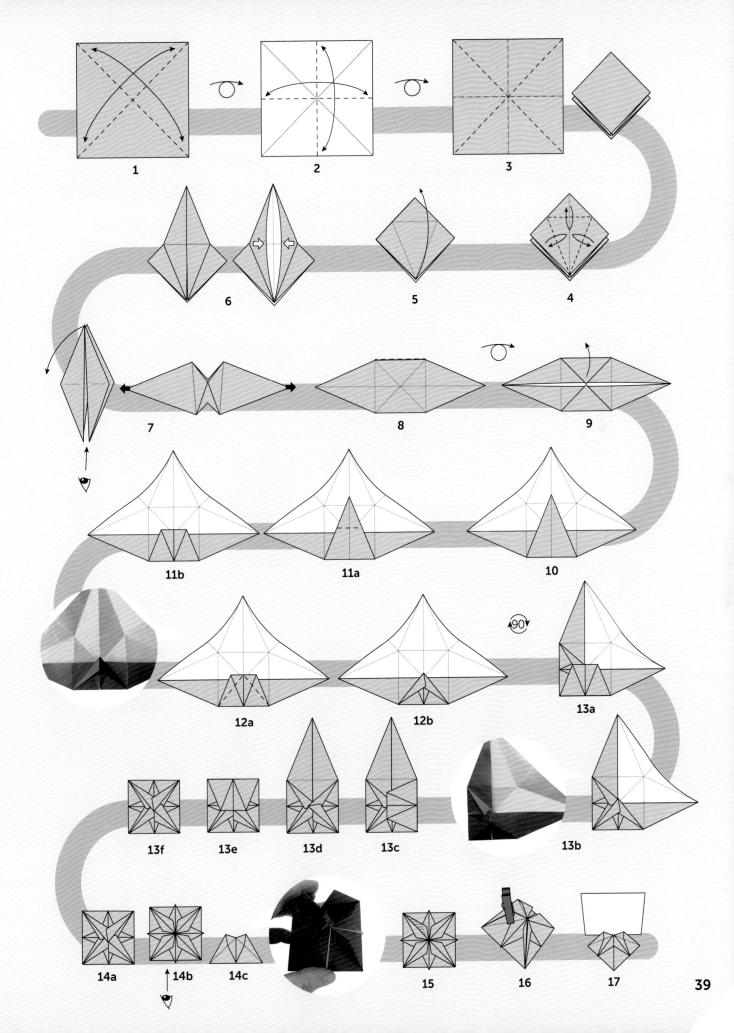

1

2

3

6

5

4

7

8

9

11b

11a

10

12a

12b

13a

13f

13e

13d

13c

13b

14a

14b

14c

15

16

17

NAPKIN RINGS
EIGHT-PETAL FLOWER

Jazz up your napkins with these intricately folded flowers that can be made in a rainbow of shades to suit your event.

Diagram by Fumika Kitagawa and Wei You

MATERIALS

- 1 sheet of 15 x 15 cm mulberry paper
- Scissors

DIFFICULTY ★★★★★

INSTRUCTIONS

1 Fold in half diagonally.

2 Bring the right half on top of the left.

3 Lift the bottom flap up to the top.

4 Repeat on the behind flap.

5 Bring the top half of the flap down to the bottom edge.

6 Flip the paper and repeat step 5 on the other side.

7 Open the paper up so that the flaps are underneath.

8 Bring the top layers over towards the centre line.

9 Open the first layer.

10 Cut off the overhanging triangle with scissors.

11 Bring over the edge flaps to the centre.

12 Cut off the overhanging triangles.

13 Unfold the paper completely. Bring the bottom corner up to the centre point.

14 Fold only between the dots.

15 Turn your paper slightly. Repeat step 14 for all the corners, rotating as you go.

16 Bring two corners up to the centre point, making a rabbit ear fold.

17 Bring the flap over to the left.

18 Fold the flap and between the dots.

19 Slightly turn the paper, and open the top flap a small bit.

20 Lift up the next corner to the centre.

21 As in steps 17–18, fold the flap over to the left.

22 Fold the bottom edge between the dots.

23 Repeat steps 19–22 for all the corners.

24 Open one flap up and bring to the left.

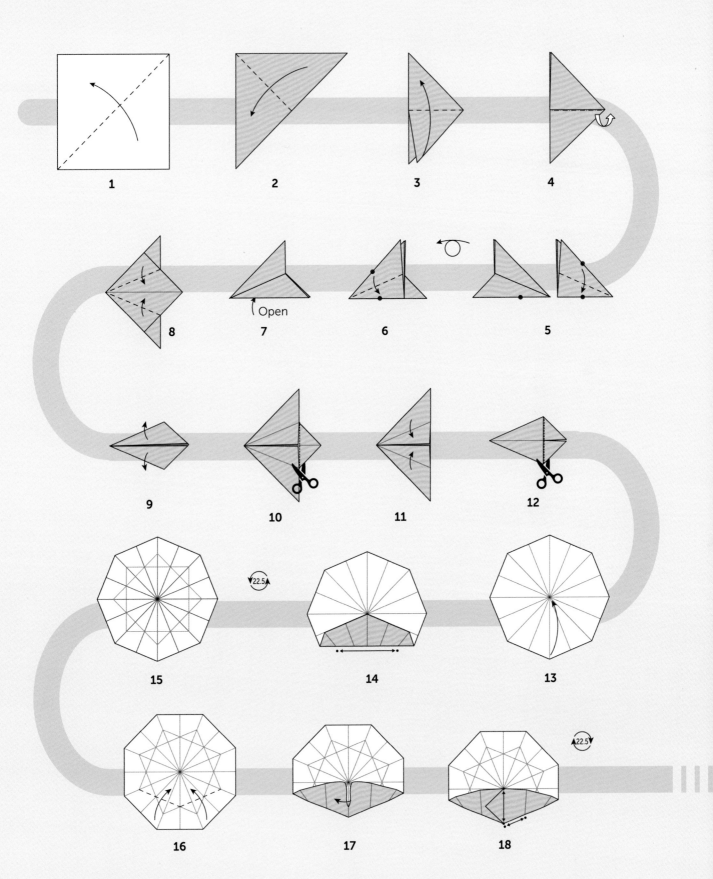

1

2

3

4

8

7 Open

6

5

9

10

11

12

15

22.5

14

13

16

17

18

22.5

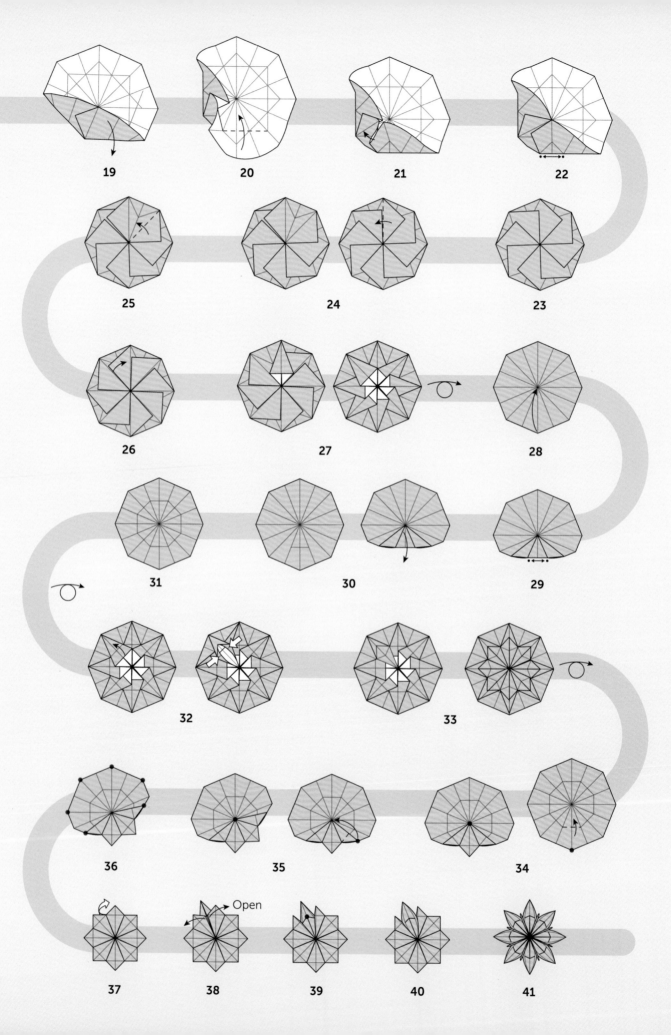

19

20

21

22

25

24

23

26

27

28

31

30

29

32

33

36

35

34

37

38

Open

39

40

41

42

25 Bring the right flap over to the left and repeat for all the flaps, moving clockwise.

26 Lift up and open one flap.

27 Squash fold the flap, lining up the fold line with the centre line. Repeat on all the flaps..

28 Turn the paper over. Bring one corner in to the centre.

29 Only fold between the dots.

30 Unfold.

31 Repeat steps 28–30 for all the corners.

32 Turn the paper over. On one triangle, lift up and fold the flap back to the crease line made in step 31, then bring the sides together to make a diamond shape.

33 Repeat step 32 for all the corners.

34 Turn the paper over. Bring the red dotted corner to the centre.

35 Bring the next corner to the centre, bringing it over the folded paper so the triangles sit next to each other.

36 Repeat step 35 to all corners shown as red dots.

37 Bring up one of the pointed flaps from behind.

38 Open up the flap to form high sides around each petal.

39 Push to flatten the folded layers to create a petal.

40 Repeat steps 37–39 to all the flaps behind.

41 Your Eight-petal Flower is now complete!

TIP

Depending on your paper, you may need to put a small bit of clear glue on the underside of each section (step 34) to keep the petals down.

Scan for a tutorial!

FLAMBOYANT FLAMINGO

These fabulous flamingo designs look best in salmon pink
and are a unique addition to any dinner party!

MATERIALS

- 1 sheet of 15 x 15 cm standard origami paper
  or other thin paper

DIFFICULTY  ★★★★★

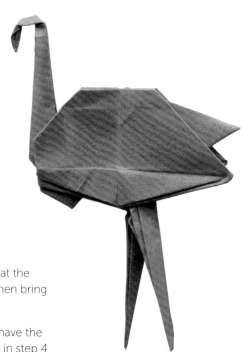

INSTRUCTIONS

1 Fold across both diagonals and unfold.

2 Flip over. Fold horizontally and vertically, then unfold.

3 Turn over. Follow the mountain creases to form a square base. The bottom point will be open.

4 Fold the top, left and right sides in towards the centre line. Unfold, then repeat on the other side.

5 Bring the top tip down to the top of the flaps, but only pinch in the middle, then unfold.

6 Bring the top tip down to the pinch line and crease well.

7 Unfold all the steps, then follow the mountain creases up to the inner square.

8 The middle should have a defined square shape. Push in the square and, using the long folded sides of your paper, gently squeeze your paper together – the mountain creases inside the square should now form a star shape inwards.

9 Flatten the paper so that the middle square sinks in, then bring the sides together.

10 Now your paper will have the valley creases you made in step 4 facing towards you.

11 Following the crease lines, lift up the top layer, then bring the sides towards the centre line.

12 Bring the top half back down. Turn the paper over, then follow step 11 but keep this side as a diamond shape.

13 Fold the top over to the left, in line with the lower edge line. Unfold, then fold the flap to the right and unfold.

14 Make a rabbit ear fold following the lower and vertical crease lines, and bring the flap to a point.

15 Bring the point to the right-hand side and flatten against the paper.

16 Fold the top-left flap over the sticking-out tail to cover it, and bring the back flap to the right.

17 Your paper should look like this – there will be two flaps on both sides.

18 Fold the tail back towards the body at a slight angle.

19 Open the tail side and rotate the paper 180 degrees.

20 Fold the paper inwards on top of the tip of the tail. Follow the creases again to bring the tail section back to the body. You will have a short tail sticking out now.

21 Rotate by 180 degrees again. Lift the front flap up past the tail.

22 Repeat with the back flap. You will be left with one left-hand flap facing down and two flaps up past the tail.

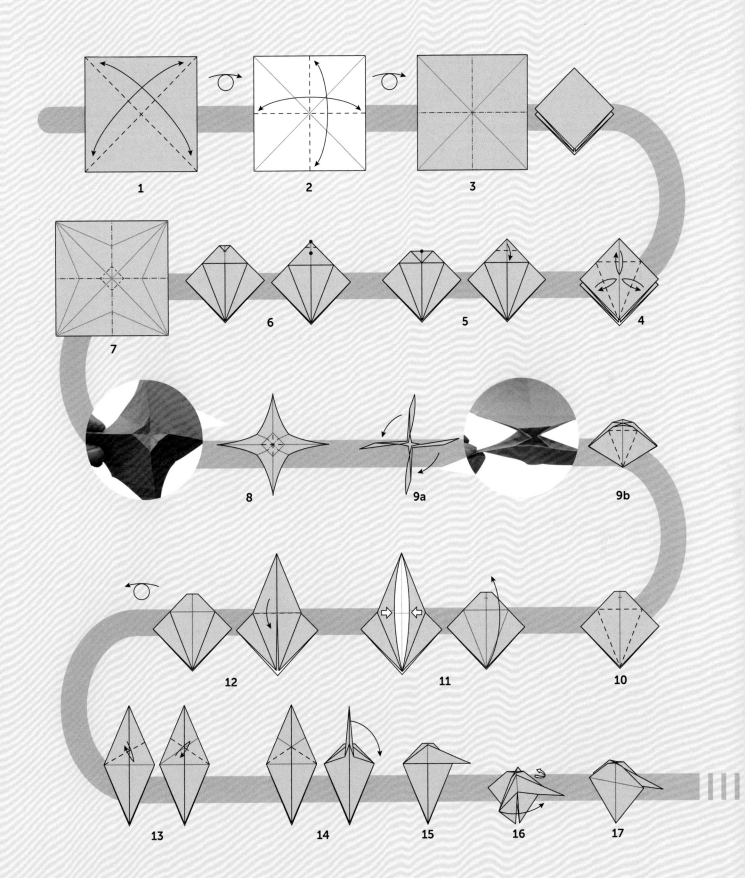

1

2

3

4

5

6

7

8

9a

9b

10

11

12

13

14

15

16

17

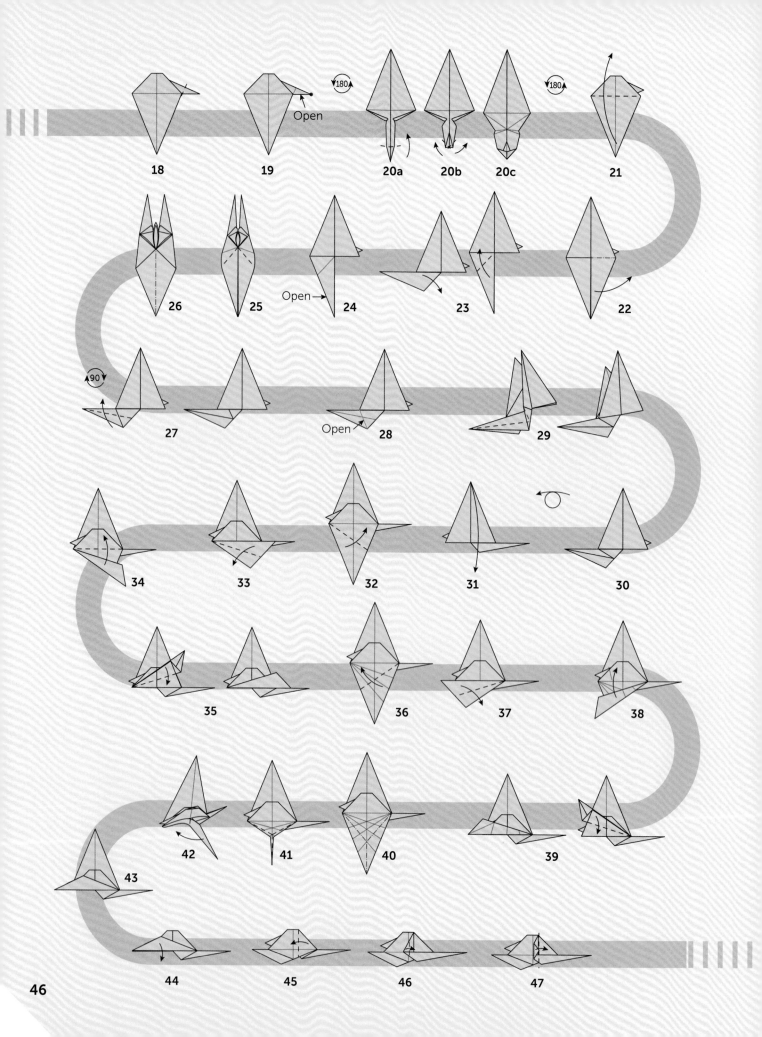

18

19

Open

20a

20b

20c

21

26

25

Open →

24

23

22

90

27

Open

28

29

34

33

32

31

30

35

36

37

38

42

41

40

39

43

44

45

46

47

23 Bring the lower flap over to the left side to the main body's bottom edge, and unfold.

24 Open at the lower flap.

25 Sharpen your valley fold lines.

26 Follow the valley lines then mountain fold along the centre line. The flap should stick out opposite the tail.

27 Rotate 90 degrees clockwise so the tail is on your right. Fold the top flap up towards the main body's bottom edge.

28 Open the flap.

29 Inside reverse fold along the creases up to the corner.

30 Turn the paper over and then repeat steps 27–29 on the other side.

31 Keep the paper with the tail to your left. Bring the front wing down.

32 Bring the wing back towards the body, folding to the right.

33 Fold the wing out on itself at a slight angle, in line with the edge of the wing.

34 Bring the folded wing back to the body.

35 Fold the wing down so that the folds are on the outside of the body, and it lines up with the bottom edge of the body.

36 Unfold the wing and then fold it back towards the body on the left.

37 Fold the wing back out on itself at a slight angle.

38 Bring the folded wing back to the body.

39 Fold the wing down so that the folds are on the outside of the body, and it lines up with the bottom edge of the body.

40 Unfold the wing then mountain fold along the first creases.

41 Following the creases, valley fold the next then mountain fold.

42 Bring the folded wing towards the tail.

43 Repeat steps 31–42 on the other wing.

44 Turn the paper back so that the tail is on the left. Bring the front wing down.

45 Fold the right-hand side of the body across the centre line so that the neck flap is extended fully.

46 Fold the corner back on itself to the crease line.

47 Bring the folded flap back. Repeat steps 45–47 on the other side on the reverse side.

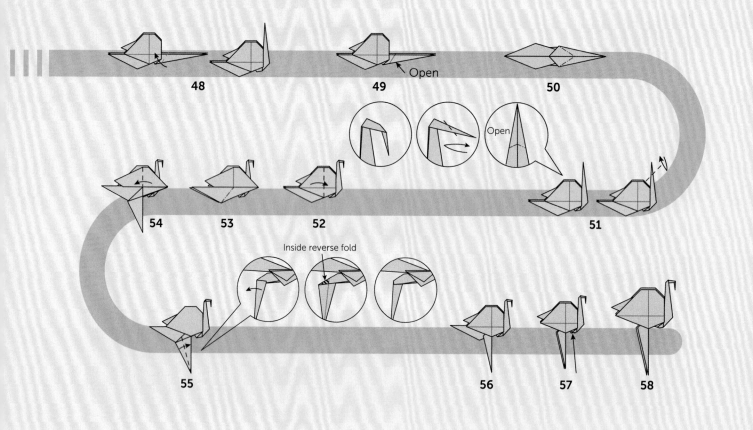

48 Open

49 Open

50

51

52

53

54

Inside reverse fold

55

56

57

58

48 Fold the neck at an angle towards the body, then unfold.

49 Open the neck flap. Following the crease lines, outside reverse fold up.

50 The bottom view of the flamingo will look like this!

51 Fold the tip of the neck at an angle and unfold. Open the flap and then outside reverse fold to make the face. On the tip of the face, fold the very tip then unfold. Open and inside reverse fold to make the beak.

52 Bring the body's left-hand front flap towards the neck.

53 Fold the lower left flap down at an angle to make the leg.

54 Bring the body flap back across the leg.

55 On the leg flap, fold the left side over the right side then unfold. Where the paper folds cross (shaded) inside reverse fold to tuck it in.

56 Repeat steps 52–55 on the other leg.

57 Valley fold and tuck in the corners under the body to tidy it up.

58 Your Flamboyant Flamingo is now finished!

TIP

The flamingo's legs can be adjusted to make other postures, such as sitting or standing on one leg.

Scan for a tutorial!

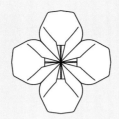

HANGING DECORATIONS

Introduction

Hanging origami decorations have seen a huge surge in popularity in wedding ceremonies. They create a romantic, dreamlike atmosphere when made in batches and hung together in an impressive display.

The origami Beautiful Blossom (see page 56) is one of the most difficult pieces in this book, but since they are just so stunning, it is hard for your hands to resist making them! Make several as they look breathtaking hanging from the ceiling over the top table at a wedding breakfast, or you could even adorn the aisle with bunches of these beautiful blossoms.

Since there are more folds involved in the flowers, I recommend using lightweight, soft and durable paper. I used white printed washi for this project, as I love the sheen that the white and silver overlay on the paper gives to the flower.

The dove is a symbol of peace and innocence, and it also symbolised love and renewal of life in ancient Greek mythology. The hanging doves are adopted from a traditional origami design, with a couple more folds added to the tail and wings. I used tant paper for the dove decorations and I had a happy afternoon tea party in mind while I created them, which inspired me to choose colours that are bright and fun yet soft to look at – accenting with cheerful colours is a wonderful way to brighten up any space.

COLOURFUL DOVES

The symbol of peace, this traditional design can be made in classic white, or why not make several in a spectrum of colours to really liven up the party?

MATERIALS

- 1 sheet of 15 x 15 cm paper (I used tant, but any type works)

DIFFICULTY ✶✶

INSTRUCTIONS

1 Fold up along the diagonal.

2 Bring the left and right corners to the top corner.

3 Bring the flaps down to the bottom corner and pinch only halfway across. Unfold.

4 Bring the side corners to the centre line.

5 Inside reverse fold following the crease lines.

6 Mountain fold in half along the vertical centre line.

7 Turn 90 degrees clockwise. Fold the front flap up, creasing on the left corner diagonal and repeat on the back flap (using the right-hand corner).

8 Folding at an angle from the top to bottom-right corner, bring the wing down. Repeat on the back flap.

9 Valley fold the whole body down towards the wing, then unfold.

10 Inside reverse fold the body, following the crease made in step 9.

11 Fold the wing up along the diagonal crease line. Repeat on the back wing.

12 Mountain fold the head then inside reverse fold to make the face. Mountain fold the tail and inside reverse fold so that only a small tail sticks out.

13 Crease the wings, using mountain folds on the top half and valley folds on the lower half to create a flared shape.

14 Your Colourful Dove is now finished!

Scan for a tutorial!

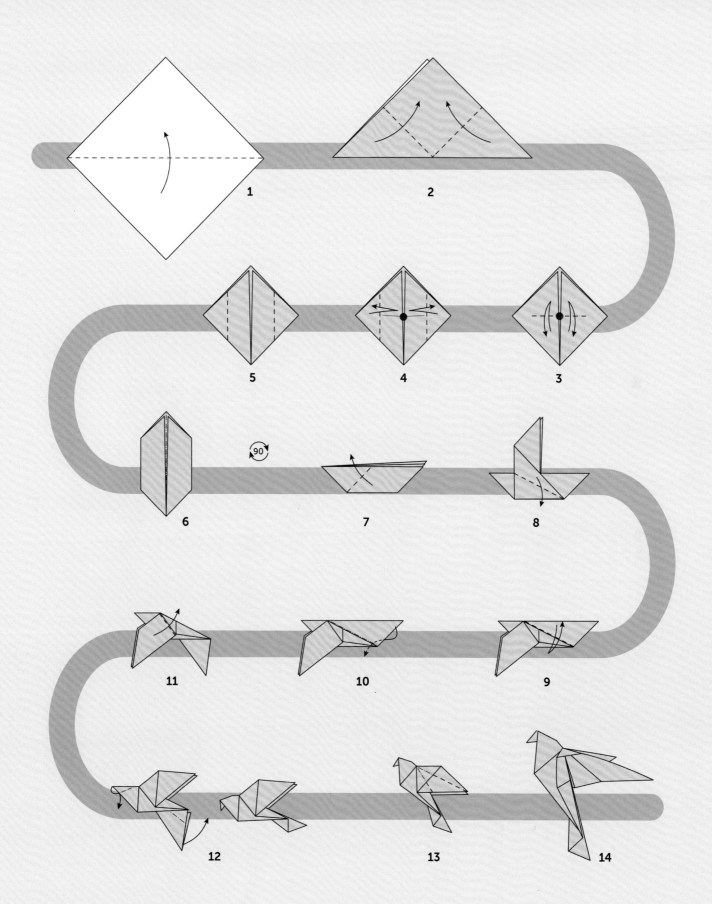

1

2

5

4

3

6

90

7

8

11

10

9

12

13

14

BEAUTIFUL BLOSSOM

These intricate blossoms look stunning when grouped together and suspended from the ceiling.

MATERIALS

- 1 sheet of 15 x 15 cm printed washi paper

DIFFICULTY ✳✳✳✳✳

INSTRUCTIONS

1 Fold on both diagonals and unfold.

2 Fold in half horizontally and vertically, then unfold.

3 Fold horizontally in half from top to bottom.

4 Fold the top flap up at an angle from the bottom-left corner to the top-right corner.

5 Your paper will look like this. Unfold it completely.

6 Fold the bottom of the paper up to where the lines cross (red dot).

7 Fold the flap down in half.

8 Bring the top half of the paper down, folding where your lines cross (red dot) so that it lines up at the bottom edge.

9 Fold the top flap up in half.

10 Fold both top flap layers towards the middle. You should see only the underside of the paper now, then unfold completely.

11 Rotate 90 degrees anticlockwise. Fold the paper up to the red dot.

12 Fold the flap down in half.

13 At the red dot, fold the rest of the paper down.

14 Fold the top flap up in half.

15 Fold the top flap layers towards the middle.

16 Unfold completely.

17 Turn the paper over. Follow the creases and sharpen the mountain folds, then turn 90 degrees, and fold along the mountain folds.

18 Valley fold the next existing creases.

19 Mountain fold the next creases.

20 It should look like this!

21 Turn the paper over. Bring the four sides (red dots) to the centre.

22 Bring the left two flaps down and flatten them, and turn 90 degrees clockwise. Repeat on the other side.

23 Bring up the lower right flap and fold at an angle to the right.

24 Repeat on all the remaining flaps. Unfold them to return back to how it looked in step 23.

25 Follow the creases and open the flaps from the centre, making a squash fold.

26 Open the back of the petal, then push out the current folds and flatten the base to create an open petal.

27 Repeat on the remaining flaps.

28 Turn the paper over. Valley fold the crease lines on the back of the blossom, bringing them together to create a star shape.

29 Pull one petal open.

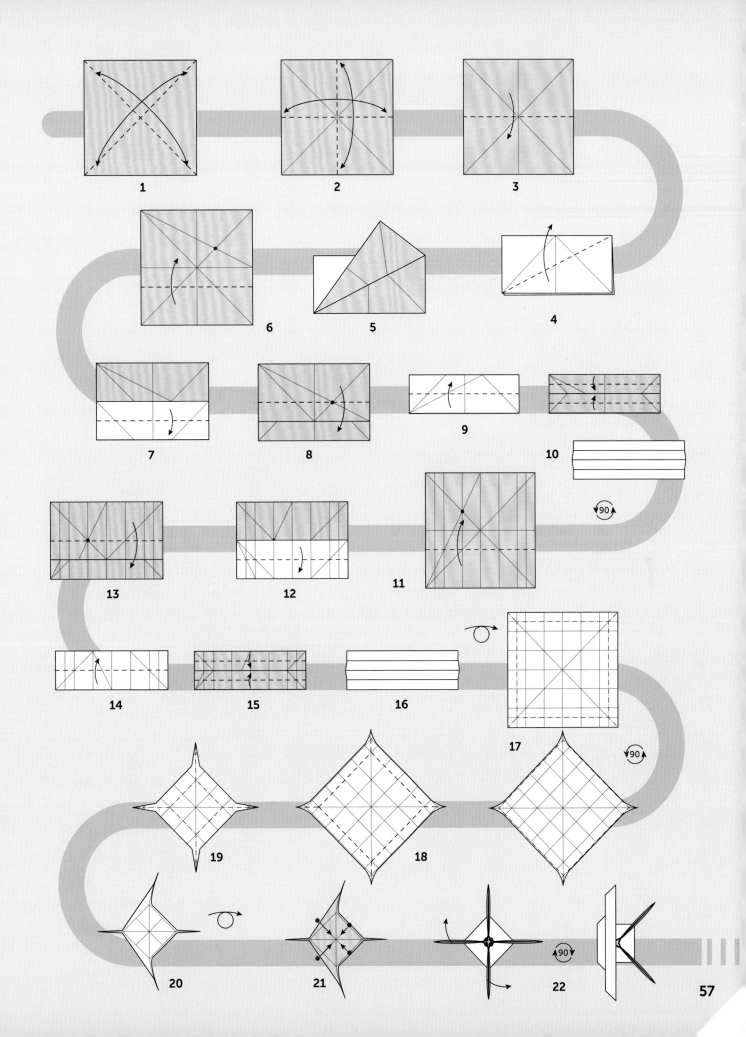

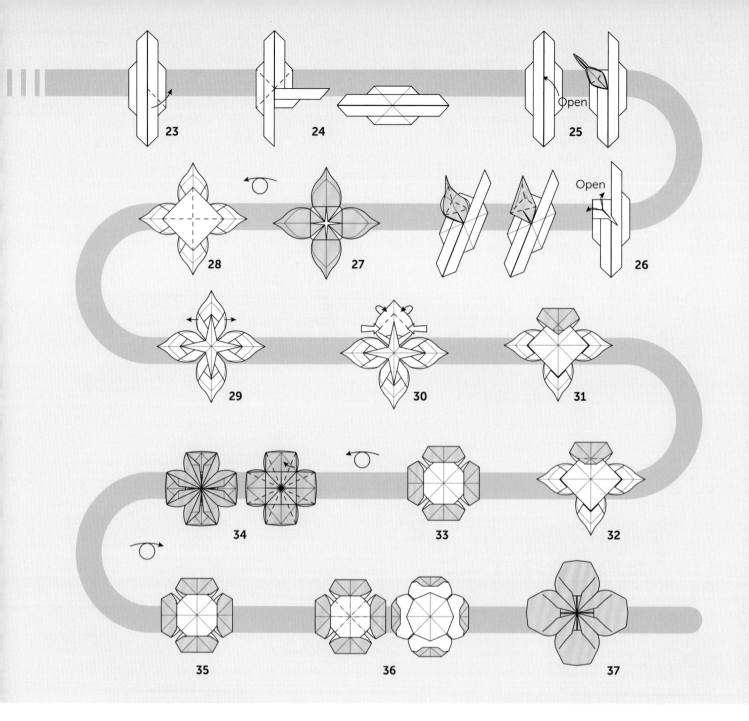

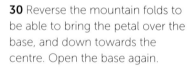
30 Reverse the mountain folds to be able to bring the petal over the base, and down towards the centre. Open the base again.

31 Mountain fold the tip of the petal back under to where your fold lines crossed.

32 Mountain fold the edge of the paper under, folding up to where the creases have crossed.

33 Repeat steps 28–32 on the other petals.

34 Turn the paper over. Fold the top flaps of each petal in towards the centre line of the petal. It doesn't matter if they don't meet the centre line exactly!

35 Turn over and round the petal edges using mountain folds.

36 Follow the mountain creases on the back plate to shape the flower. This brings the petals together so round them out a little until you have a soft edge on each.

37 Your Beautiful Blossom is now finished!

TIP

To hang, thread a needle with a thin thread or cotton and poke through the centre of the blossom, knot under it to secure in place then continue with more blossoms!

Scan for a tutorial!

WALL ART

Introduction

Paper art panels are becoming increasingly popular for all kinds of events. Kirigami flowers and butterflies are never out of fashion. When the templates are available and the technique is simple, you will find yourself absentmindedly making them from any pieces of paper you find lying around!

You can be as creative as you like when designing your wall art, arranging a multitude of pieces in different sizes and colours to suit the room or occasion. The flowers in the Rose Wall Panel (see page 62) would make a pretty display for a wedding or Valentine's Day. I used screen-printed washi with a subtle pattern for this panel, which adds some shine without distracting the eye from the overall look. The Brilliant Butterflies (see page 65) would look gorgeous in bright colours at a springtime party, and it would be lovely to use the origami Square Flowers to spell out a child's name in a bedroom.

Square Flowers are brought into this chapter as an opening to the next section on tiles (see page 66). The idea of connecting them to make a geometric panel is inspired by Japanese *shippou*, in which the circumferences of multiple circles are overlapped by a quarter at top, bottom, left and right to make a continual pattern. The overlapping circles symbolise the meaning of 'happy ending'. This will create a quiet and calm backdrop for any lover of minimalism.

ROSE WALL PANEL

These stemless roses are so simple to make. Together they create an effective three-dimensional wall panel that would be a great gift for a loved one.

MATERIALS
- 3 or more sheets of pink A4 (110gsm) paper for the petals, 1 sheet of white or green A4 paper for the leaves
- Pen
- Scissors
- Wooden pegs
- Clear glue
- Wooden skewers

PATTERNS
- Petals: P1, P2, P3, P4, P5, P6 (see page 156)
- Leaves: L1, L2, L3 (see page 156)

DIFFICULTY ✳︎✳︎✳︎

INSTRUCTIONS

1 Using the rose petal templates, cut out two petals of each size.

2 Make a small cut (less than 1 cm) at the centre of the base of each petal.

3 Apply glue to one side of the cut and make a curve at the base of each petal. Use a peg to hold the glued area until dry.

4 Curve the petals using a wooden skewer. For the smaller-sized petals, curve inwards on one side only.

5 Use three of the smallest-sized petals to a make a closed cup. Apply clear glue to hold them together and use a wooden skewer to hold the centre of the flower secure to keep its shape until the glue has dried.

6 Gradually glue more petals in place at the base of the rose to build up the flower shape.

7 For the middle-sized petals, press the bottom curve to make it flatter, changing the angle of the petals to open them up more. Gently curve the petals on both sides and continue to add to the rose, as in step 6.

8 Repeat to add larger petals to the outer edge. Continue to add petals until your rose is your desired size.

9 Your finished rose should look like this!

10 Attach a leaf at the base, if required, by cutting from the leaf template, folding down the centre and gluing onto the back of the rose. You can also cut out a leaf shape on a light-coloured paper, and use individual roses as place card holders.

TIP
For best results, wait until the previous petal is fixed in place before sticking on a new petal.

1

2

3a

3b

4

5a

5b

6a

6b

7a

7b

8

9

10

BRILLIANT BUTTERFLIES

Cutting out these butterfly shapes couldn't be easier and they make a great addition to any nursery or garden room.

MATERIALS

- 110 gsm coloured paper in any size (A4 is readily available)
- Pen
- Scissors

PATTERNS

- Big butterfly and small butterfly templates (see page 157)

DIFFICULTY ✳

INSTRUCTIONS

1 Use the template to draw around the small or big butterfly shape on your selected paper. It is easier to fold the butterfly in half and cut the shape from folded paper.

2 Cut round the butterfly shape using scissors.

3 Your finished butterfly should look like this!

TIP
Use glue dots or damage-free paste to fix the butterflies onto walls or other surfaces.

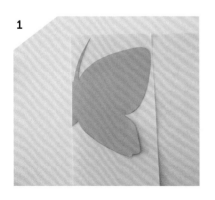

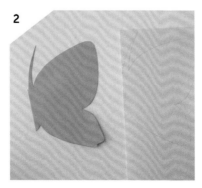

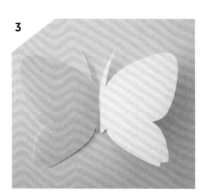

SQUARE FLOWERS

Use these flowers to spell out a name or a word of your choice, or tessellate them to form a striking *shippou*-inspired pattern.

MATERIALS

- 1 sheet of 15 x 15 cm Yuzen washi paper

DIFFICULTY ★★★★

INSTRUCTIONS

1 Fold in half horizontally and vertically and unfold.

2 Fold your paper up diagonally.

3 Bring the corner of the top flap down and pinch the middle, then unfold.

4 Fold the bottom edge up to the pinch line and unfold.

5 Fold the bottom edge up to the fold line you made in step 4 and unfold.

6 Unfold your paper and repeat steps 2–5 along the other diagonal, then turn your paper over. It should look like this.

7 Fold the bottom half of the paper up to where your lines cross at the top (red dot), then unfold.

8 Repeat on the top, right and left sides, folding each to the opposite crossing lines (red dot).

9 Sharpen the outer creases to make a diamond.

10 Mountain fold the outer straight lines.

11 Pinch along the straight lines and outer diamond, then push in and valley fold the inner diamond. You should have a star shape from your leftover fold lines. Use the valley fold lines (from step 8) along the sides of your four mountain folds to flatten the bottom of your paper so it looks like 11d. Your paper should be a square shape with the four raised flaps, and if you look on the underside, you will have a diamond nestled between 4 squares.

12 On the right-hand side, open your raised flap and mountain fold along your second crease line, and valley fold your central straight line.

13 Mountain fold up along the outer crease line.

14 Look at the side you just folded. Bring the bottom edge up while you close the flap. It will now be tucked in.

15 Repeat steps 12–14 on all the remaining flaps.

16 Open the small flap and then squash fold, bringing the edge to the centre.

17 Repeat on the remaining flaps. Your Square Flower is now complete!

Scan for a tutorial!

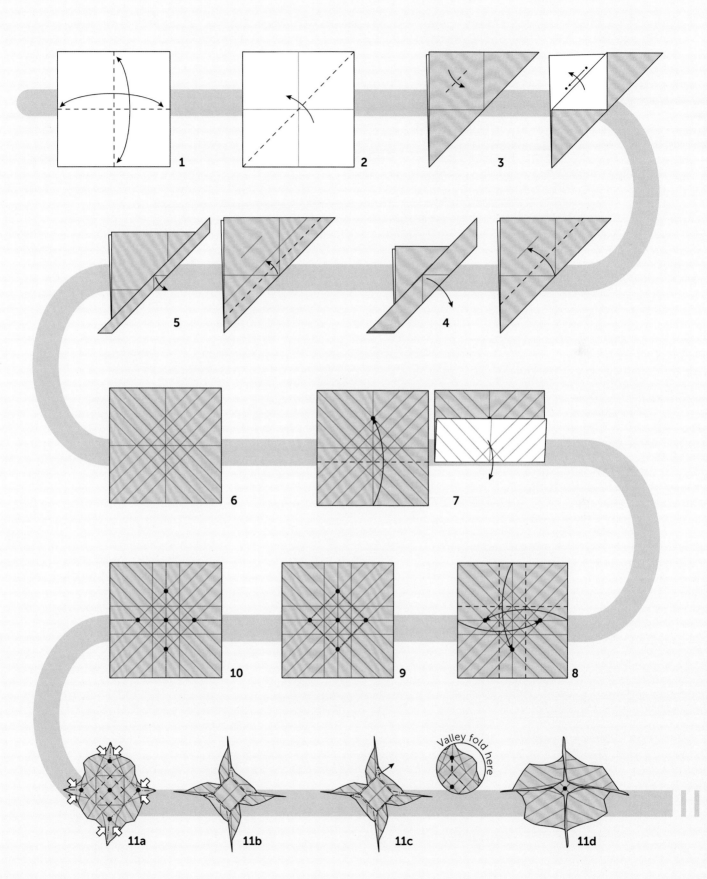

1

2

3

5

4

6

7

10

9

8

Valley fold here

11a

11b

11c

11d

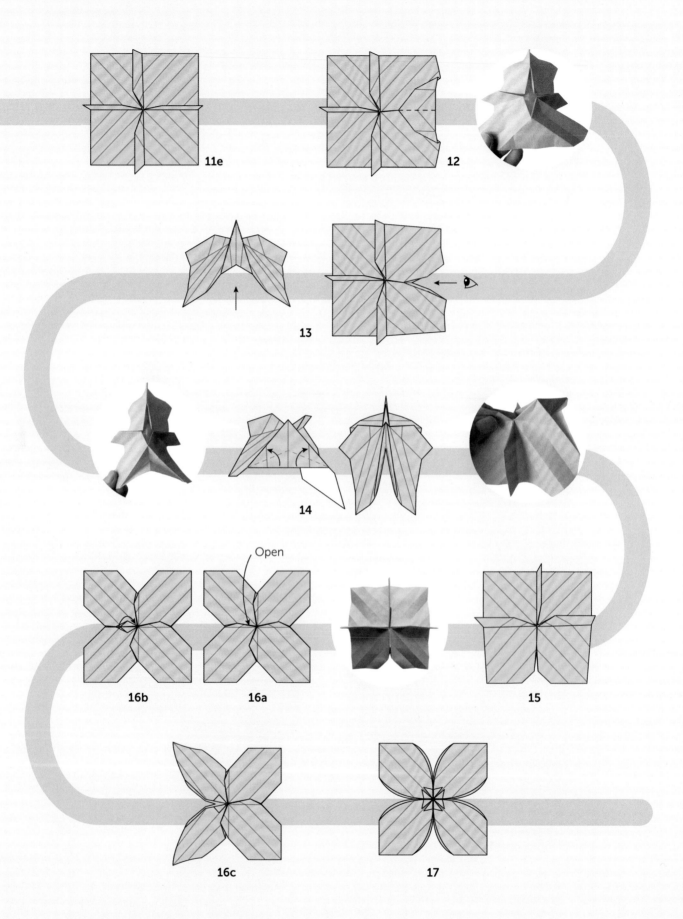

11e

12

13

14

Open

16b

16a

15

16c

17

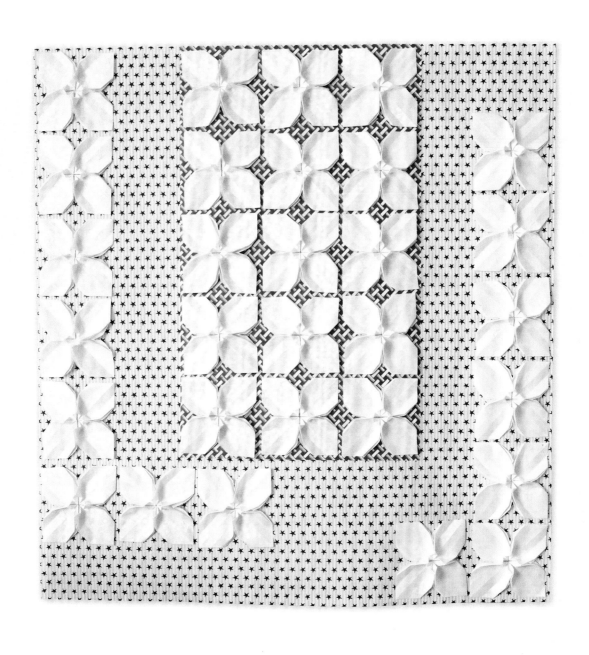

TILES

Introduction

The technique of making origami tiles is simple, but it results in a highly intricate and luxurious look, from a small piece of framed art to a large-scale wall art installation. Tiles were an easy start when I wanted to create my own origami designs. They begin with a simple origami base that can be decorated with any variation design of your choice. Most are vertically, horizontally and diagonally symmetrical, which makes it easy to place them together to create a panel, and many complex paper art installations are made from duplicates of easy-to-make pieces.

Patterned washi and tant paper are my top choices for making origami tiles; the paper is tough enough to handle the repeat folds and there are so many colours and patterns to experiment with, which are hard to resist. The fun part is playing around with patterns – you can really get creative making unique art pieces that will surprise any recipient.

Origami tiling can be a great way to relax and meditate. Once you have learned how to make a piece you can continue to make as many as you want, and the repetitive movements allow you to simply be in the moment, focusing on the texture of the paper and the feel of each fold, calming your mind while your thoughts and worries drift away. It also allows you to teach other people that piece, which can be a great bonding activity to enjoy with family and friends.

WINDMILL TILES

So simple to fold, these quick-to-make windmill tiles look lovely when made in contrasting colours and presented in a frame.

MATERIALS

- For the white, blue, black and brown design: 1 sheet of 9 x 9 cm Yuzen paper per tile
- For the pink and beige design on page 2: 1 sheet of 7.5 x 7.5 cm tant paper per tile

DIFFICULTY ✳✳

INSTRUCTIONS

1 Fold in half and unfold.

2 Fold the top and bottom edges to the centre line and unfold.

3 Fold along the centre vertically and unfold.

4 Fold the left and right edges to the centre line and unfold.

5 Turn over. Fold each corner to the centre point and unfold.

6 Turn over. Fold the tip of each corner to the first fold line.

7 Fold diagonally and unfold.

8 Turn 90 degrees anticlockwise. Rabbit ear fold at the lines. The corner should stand up.

9 Fold the sticking-up corner down to the left. Lift up the right-hand edge, opening the inner flap of this corner as you bring the edge over (green dot).

10 Bring the right-hand side over the opened flap and flatten. You should now have two points sticking out.

11 Fold the remaining side open along your diagonal crease lines so that it stands up.

12 Rotate 90 degrees clockwise. Fold the open side down along your crease line to meet the centre line.

13 Lift the flap closest to your first flap and fold diagonally back for a four-pointed tile.

14 Shape the windmill blades as desired by wiggling open the 4 points with your finger. Your Windmill Tile is now complete!

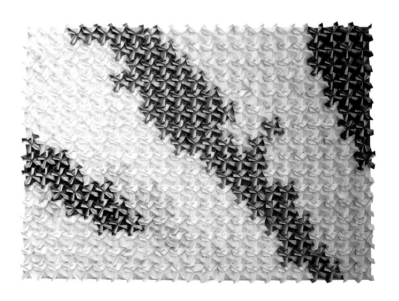

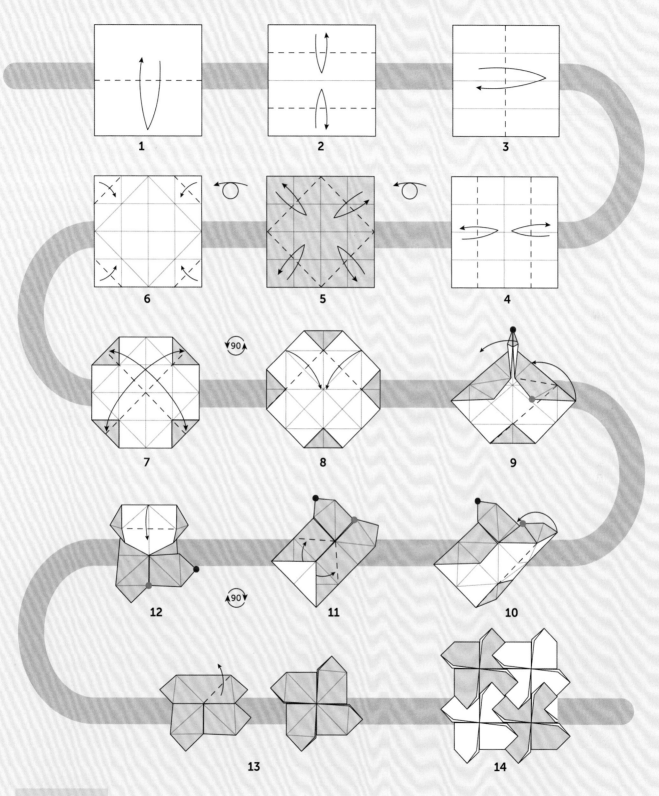

DIAMOND TILES

Making these diamond tiles is so therapeutic it becomes addictive!
Combine two contrasting colours for an eye-catching design.

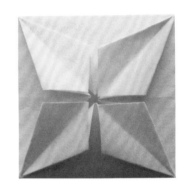

MATERIALS

- 1 sheet of 7 x 7 cm Yuzen washi paper per tile

DIFFICULTY ✱✱

INSTRUCTIONS

1 Fold in half and unfold.

2 Fold the top and bottom edges in to the centre line and unfold.

3 Turn 90 degrees anticlockwise and repeat steps 1–2.

4 Turn the paper over. Fold each corner to the centre point and unfold.

5 Turn the paper over. Follow the existing creases and bring the four marked points to the centre. It will look like 5c, then flatten down the top flaps.

6 On the top-right square, fold the left diagonal on top of the right.

7 Fold over the top flap back to the centre line.

8 Bring the left folded flap back to its original place.

9 On the same square, fold the right diagonal over to the left.

10 Fold over the top flap back to the centre line.

11 Bring the right folded flap back to its original place.

12 The top square should look like this! Repeat steps 6–11 on the remaining three squares.

13 Your Diamond Tile is now complete!

14 To join the tiles together, insert the corner of one tile (blue outline) into the side pocket of another tile (green outline). Bring the upper flap (red outline) onto the top.

15 Keep joining your tiles together in this way to create your own design.

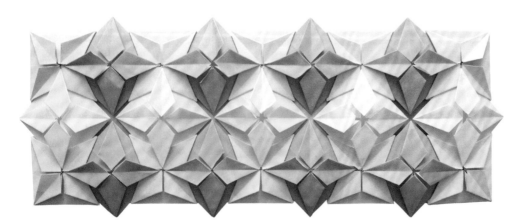

Scan for a tutorial!

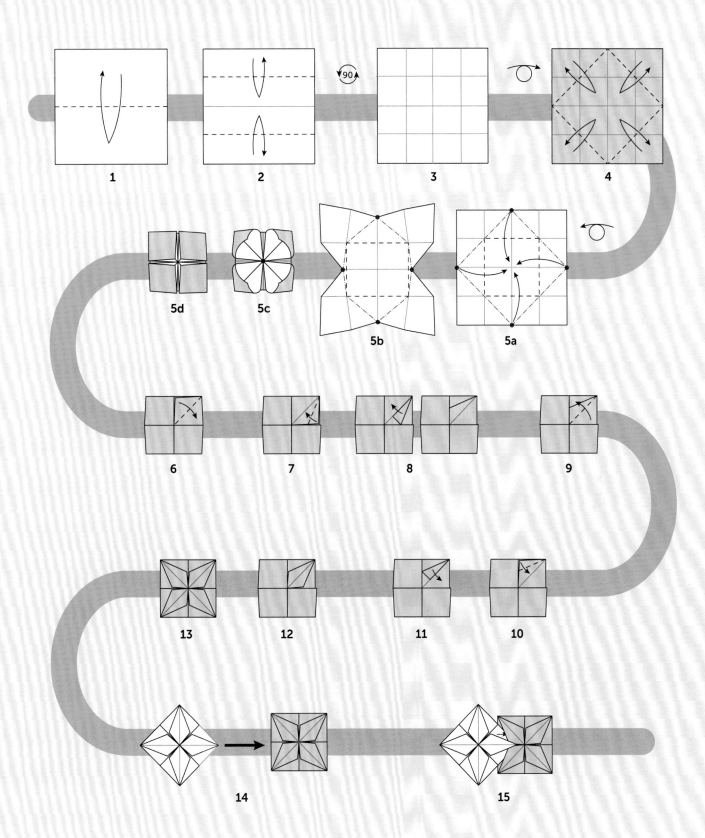

SQUARE FLOWER TILES

The Yuzen washi paper's tan base colour is enhanced by subtle blues and greens that sink into the base tone, topped with a rich gold pattern that brings up the red and white hues (see page 78). The pattern is taken from vintage fabric, giving it a luxury feel.

MATERIALS
- 1 sheet of 15 x 15 cm Yuzen washi paper per tile

DIFFICULTY ★★★★

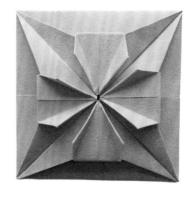

INSTRUCTIONS

1 Fold across both diagonals and unfold.

2 Flip over. Fold in half horizontally and vertically, then unfold.

3 Turn over. Follow the mountain creases to form a square base. The bottom point will be open.

4 Bring the top, left and right corners of the top layer to the centre line and unfold.

5 Lift up the top layer, following the creases.

6 Bring the sides to the centre line and squash. A new diamond shape is formed. Repeat steps 4–6 on the other side.

7 Looking underneath, keep the folds on the flaps and open the middle section.

8 Sharpen the square's edges.

9 Turn the paper over. Open up the top half of the paper.

10 Flatten the lower flap up towards the open paper.

11 Following the creases you made in step 10 (on the back of the flap), bring the flap down diagonally to the left and right.

12 Follow the creases to start a rabbit ear fold on the flap.

13 Flatten the bottom of the flap, then bring the point of the flap over to the right.

14 Your paper should look like this.

15 Bring the flap up, then squash fold the tip.

16 It should look like this. Repeat steps 10–15 on the flap opposite.

17 Your paper should look like this.

18 Turn the paper 90 degrees clockwise. Bring the right-hand flap towards the centre, opening out the sides as you fold.

19 Place over the current points. Repeat steps 18–19 on the remaining flaps.

20 It should look like this.

21 Following the crease lines, tuck in the shadowed areas clockwise. Don't tuck two shadowed areas under one flap. Repeat on the left side.

22 Mountain fold each point and tuck behind into the pockets.

23 It should look like this.

24 Shape the flower petals with creases along the sides of each.

25 Your Square Flower Tile is now finished!

Scan for a tutorial!

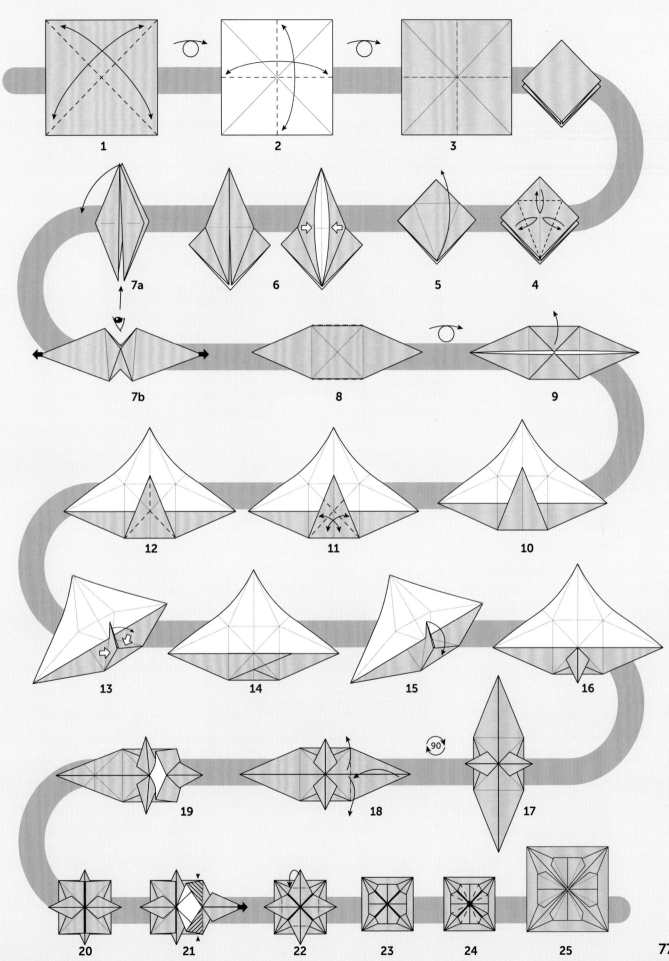

1

2

3

7a

6

5

4

7b

8

9

12

11

10

13

14

15

16

19

18

17

20

21

22

23

24

25

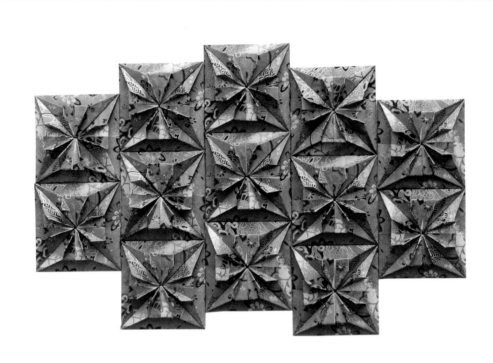

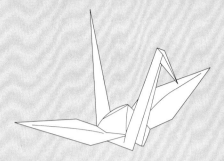

PAPER GIFTS

Introduction

Paper gifts are not just for a first wedding anniversary! People have become fascinated by origami and kirigami designs, and paper art has become popular for any occasion. If you are looking for handmade gift ideas, papercraft is more beginner-friendly than other art forms and the creative opportunities that it offers are endless.

This chapter is all about birds and flowers, which, for many, are symbols of beauty, love and hope. The Feathered Crane (see page 84) can be made from a variety of papers using the simple feather template, and some variation ideas are given in this chapter. The paper crane (折鶴 *orizuru*) is one of the classic origami designs in Japanese culture. Thousand cranes (千羽鶴 *senbazuru*) is from a classic story based on the life of Sadako Sasaki, which states that one wish is granted if someone folds a thousand cranes. But one made with love is a perfect gift.

My inspiration for making feathers came from traditional Asian art and nature. The first feathered crane I made was some years ago while I was working on a Ukiyo-e (浮世絵) project to decorate a Japanese-themed British gastropub. Ukiyo-e (translated as: 'picture(s) of the floating world') is the Japanese woodblock print or painting of landscape, people's lives and tales from the seventeenth century. While I was checking on the traditional kirigami art displays, I spotted boxes of scrap paper in the studio room that were too pretty to throw away, so I cut them into feather shapes and attached them to a painted crane to decorate the artwork and reveal the beauty of the paper. Pop colours and different medias are used in this project to bring traditional Japanese culture closer to modern life.

Paper flowers, such as the Romantic Rose (see page 91), are taking over as the must-have wedding and anniversary decoration or gift. The petal template is available in seven sizes to create intricate and lifelike flowers, and they can also be simplified to fit the modern minimalist style.

An origami Proud Parrot (see page 94) completes this chapter, which is a project with a little challenge, using paper tessellation to create the wings. The beauty of the end result makes the effort that goes into them worthwhile.

CRANES
BASIC CRANE

In Japanese tradition, the crane stands for good fortune and longevity because of its fabled lifespan of a thousand years.

MATERIALS
- 1 sheet of 15 x 15 cm tant paper, around 110 gsm (or any other paper suitable for folding)

DIFFICULTY ✳✳

TIP
Do not use standard origami paper for the Basic Crane. It is too light and won't be able to keep its shape after all the gluing.

INSTRUCTIONS

1 Fold across both diagonals and unfold.

2 Flip over. Fold in half horizontally and vertically, then unfold.

3 Turn over. Follow the mountain creases to form a square base. The bottom point will be open.

4 Lift the side corners of the top layer and fold so the sides meet in the centre. Lift and fold the top corner down, then unfold.

5 Lift up the top layer and follow the existing creases to bring the sides towards the middle. It will look like step 6.

6 Bring the sides to the centre line and squash. A new diamond shape is formed. Repeat steps 4–6 on the other side.

7 Lift the side corners on the top layer and fold so the sides meet in the centre and repeat on the back.

8 Fold the two bottom flaps up and unfold.

9 Open the left-hand side, lift up the lower flap and inside reverse fold. Repeat on the other side. This forms the head and tail of your crane.

10 Fold one tip at an angle then inside reverse fold to make the crane's head.

11 Fold the wings out and shape as preferred.

12 Your crane is now complete!

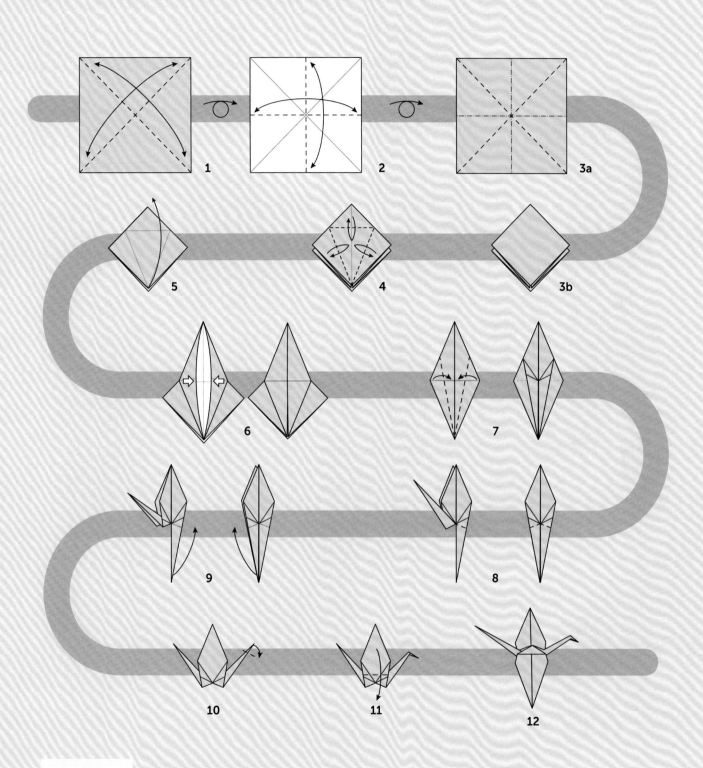

1

2

3a

5

4

3b

6

7

9

8

10

11

12

Scan for a tutorial!

FEATHERED CRANE

This design was inspired by a vintage feather fan. I really enjoyed playing with the colours and arranging the feathers.

MATERIALS

- 1 sheet of 15 x 15 cm 110 gsm paper for the crane
- Watercolour 200 gsm paper
- Coloured 80–100 gsm paper in a range of colours
- Metallic acrylic paint
- Paintbrush
- Scissors or Cricut
- Bamboo stick
- Tacky or clear glue

PATTERNS

- 4 x A7, 4 x A8, 6 x A9 feathers (see page 157)
- 24 x Type B feathers (see page 157)
  – use a mix of all three sizes so
  you can see which look the best

DIFFICULTY ✷✷

TIP

It is much easier to use a bamboo stick to curve the feathers as well as to hold them in position while the glue dries!

INSTRUCTIONS

1 Fold a Basic Crane (see page 82) and flatten down the bottom part so it can stand.

2 Cut out all of the feathers using scissors or Cricut. Use watercolour paper for the type A feathers and coloured paper for the type B feathers.

3 Paint the type A feathers using one colour for all the sizes.

4 Once dry, curve the type A feathers in half using a bamboo stick.

5 The curved feathers should look like this.

6 Fold all of the type B feathers in half.

7 Carefully cut lots of fine lines into the type B feathers, starting from the bottom towards the tip. Angle your scissors down towards the fold line.

8 Open up the type B feathers and gently curl them downwards.

9 Fully open up the crane's wings.

10 Apply some glue to the bottom of the type B feathers and stick them onto the back edge of the wings.

11 Pay attention to the overall shape of the wings while gluing on.

12 Once all of the type B feathers are in place, you are now ready to add the rest of the feathers. Apply some glue to the bottom of the type A feathers and place the smallest feathers closest to the crane's body, moving up to the largest ones at the edge of the wings. Make sure to slightly overlap them as you go.

13 Your Feathered Crane is now finished!

1

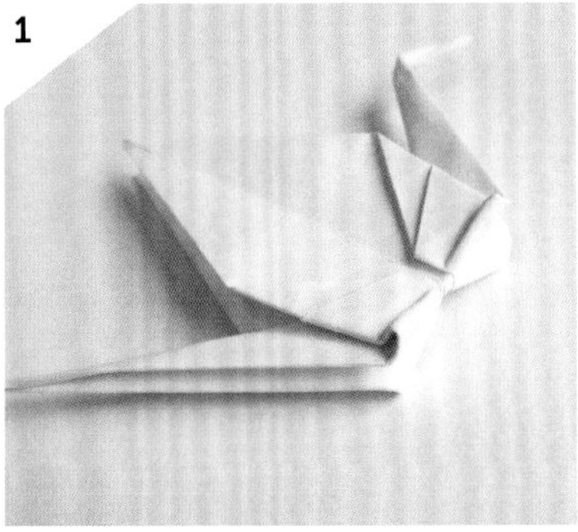

2

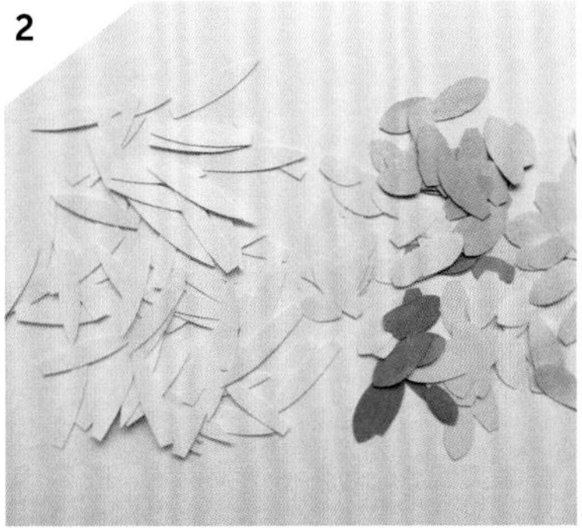

3

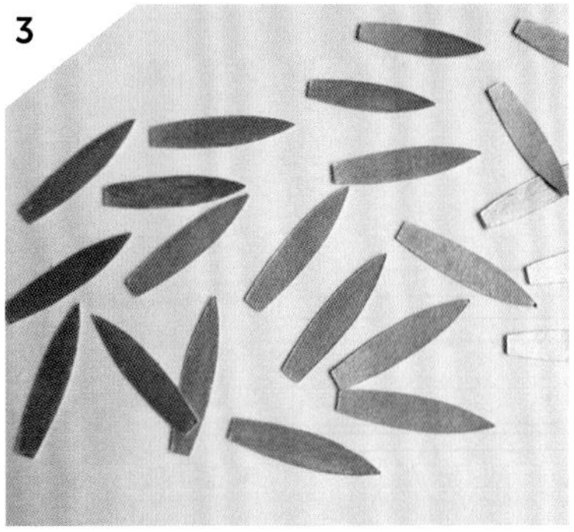

4

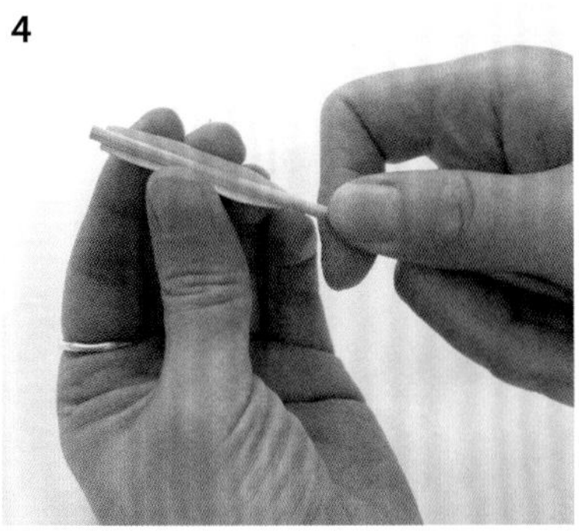

5

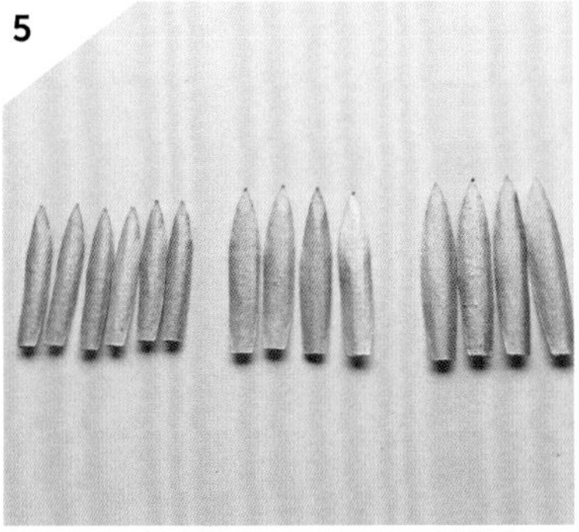

6

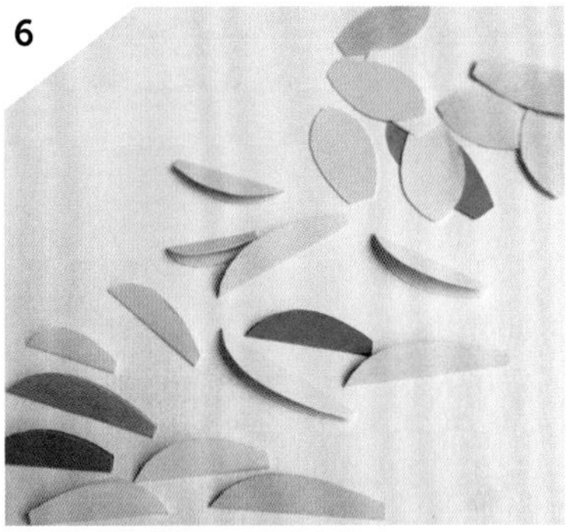

7

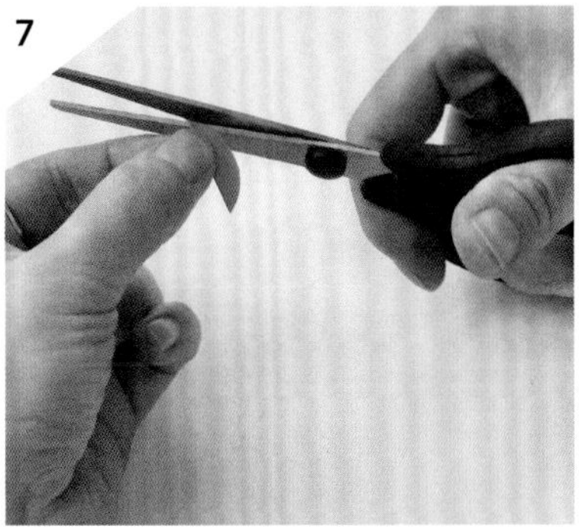

8

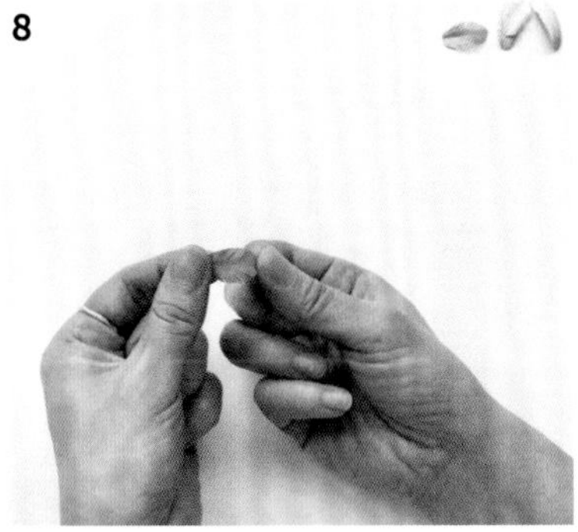

9

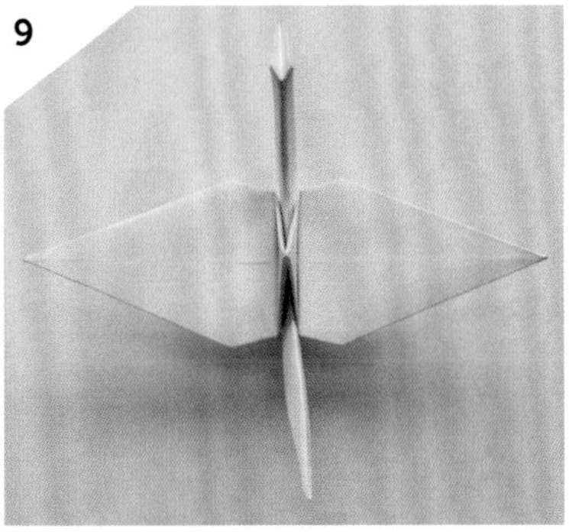

10

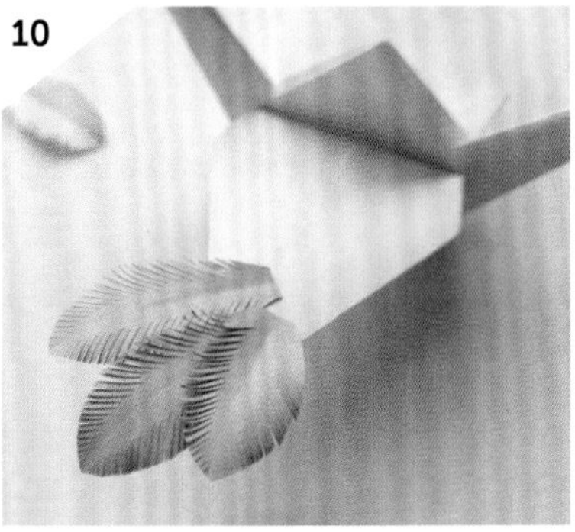

11

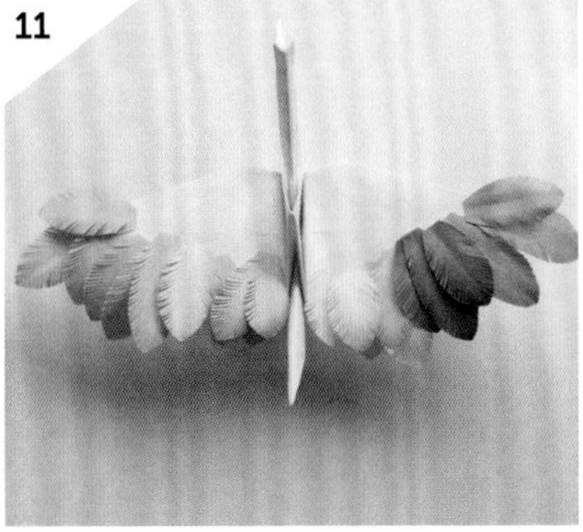

12a

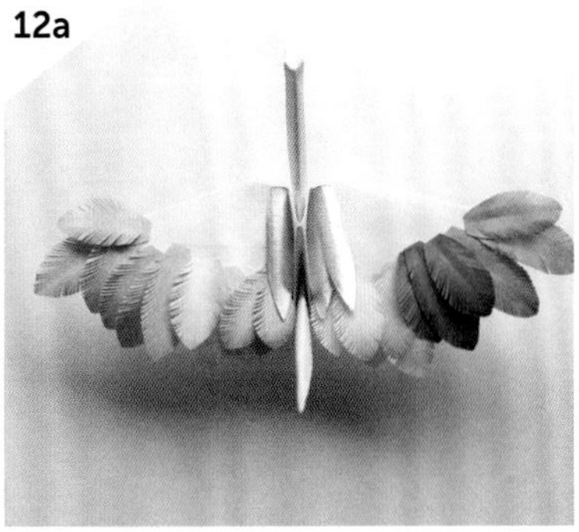

12b

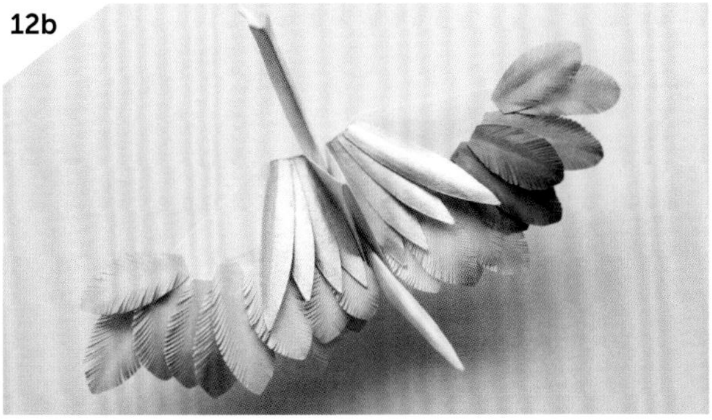

13

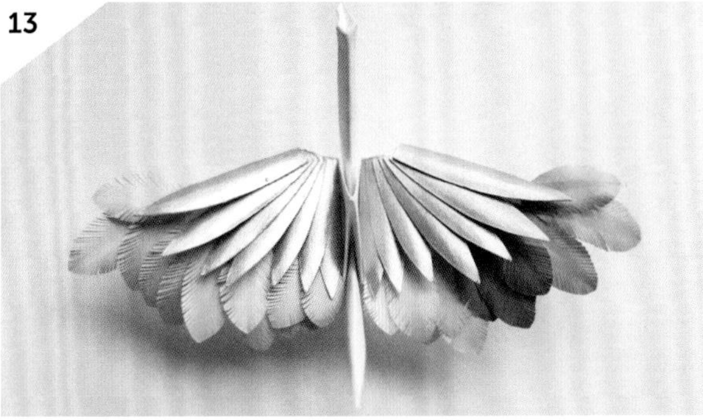

SANDHILL CRANE

This design is inspired by the sandhill crane – large long-legged birds
that have a red crown and grey body, sometimes with rusty staining.

MATERIALS

- 1 sheet of 15 x 15 cm 110 gsm paper for the crane
- Watercolour 200 gsm paper
- Watercolour paint and paintbrush
- Tacky or clear glue
- Scissors

PATTERNS

- 12 x A8, 12 x A9 feathers (see page 157)
  30 x B2, 10 x B3 feathers (see page 157)

DIFFICULTY ✳✳

TIP

Pick one or two main
colours for your crane.
Here I've used tan and
blue as the key colours,
adding red and
yellow to the feathers to
create different tones.

INSTRUCTIONS

1 Cut out 12 x A8 and 12 x A9
feathers and 30 x B2 and 10 x B3
feathers from the watercolour
paper. Apply watercolour paint to
the feathers, layer by layer rather
than in one coat.

2 Paint the crane's paper to match
the wings.

3 Fold a Basic Crane (see page 82).

4 Once dry, cut small lines on the
middle of both sides of the type A
feather. Gently curve the type A
feathers in half using your hands.

5 Cut fine lines into the type B
feathers, starting at the bottom and
cutting at a downward angle.

6 Apply glue to the bottom of the
feathers and arrange them onto
the crane. Place some type B
feathers closest to the crane's body

and then add in type A feathers.
Build up the layers in this way until
you have only type B feathers left,
which can be layered on the rest
of the crane's body.

7 Your Sandhill Crane is now
finished!

1

2

3a

3b

4a

4b

5a

5b

5c

6a

6b

7

EXOTIC CRANE

The technique of adding feathers to cranes is simple, which allows us to put more thought into creating original colour combinations and designs.

MATERIALS

- 1 sheet of 15 x 15 cm 110 gsm paper for the crane
- Approximately two sheets of paper from old magazines (tear off your desired colours and patterns)
- Tacky or clear glue   •   Scissors   •   Bamboo stick

PATTERNS

- Type A feathers (see page 157) – prepare around six of each pattern, depending on how full you want the feather design to look

DIFFICULTY   ✷✷

INSTRUCTIONS

1 Cut out some pieces from magazines. Mix and match the colours and patterns.

2 Fold a Basic Crane (see page 82).

3 Draw the type A feather shapes in pencil onto the reverse side of the magazine pages. Divide the feathers by colours or by sizes in the order you prefer.

4 Fold the feathers in the middle.

5 Apply glue to the bottom edge of the feathers, and start placing the feathers onto the crane. Put the smaller feathers closer to the body.

6 You can either make the wings broader by gluing the feathers flat...

7 ... Or increase the three-dimensional height of the feathers by keeping them half-folded when gluing.

8 Use a bamboo stick to secure the feathers when gluing. Pay closer attention to the overall shape of the wings rather than laying the feathers out symmetrically.

9 Now the wings should be covered with feathers.

10 Add in extra feathers to adjust the overall shape and make the wing look fuller.

11 Your Exotic Crane is now finished!

TIP
This white blush crane is made from tant paper using type A feathers and adding in extra smaller feathers. See the Tant Crane on page 90 for a similar heavily feathered crane.

1

2

3

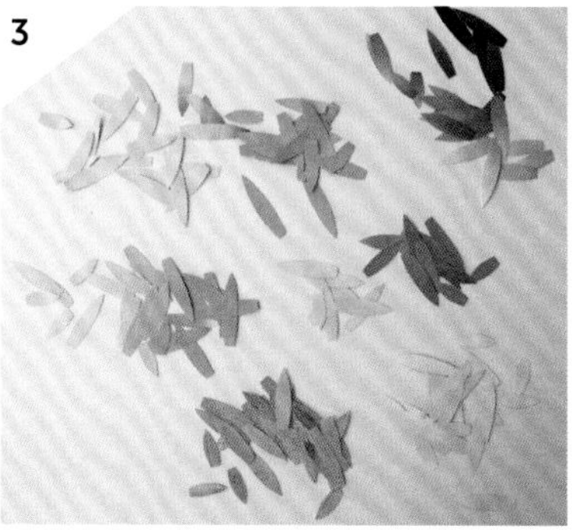

4

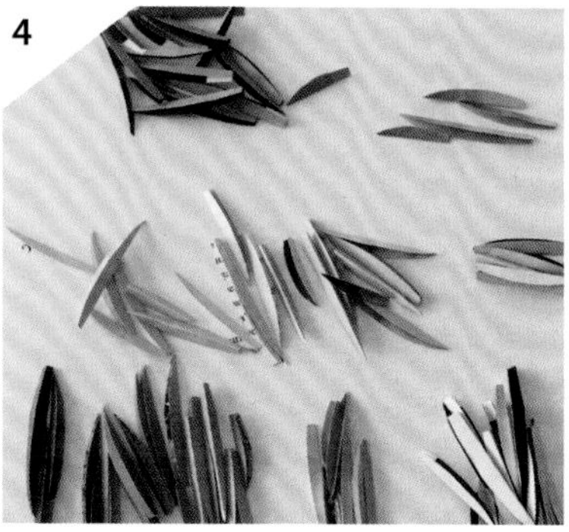

5a

5b

6a

6b

7a

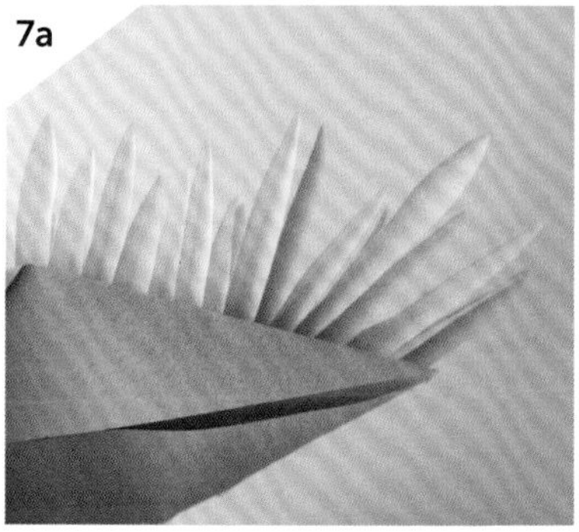

7b

8a

8b

9

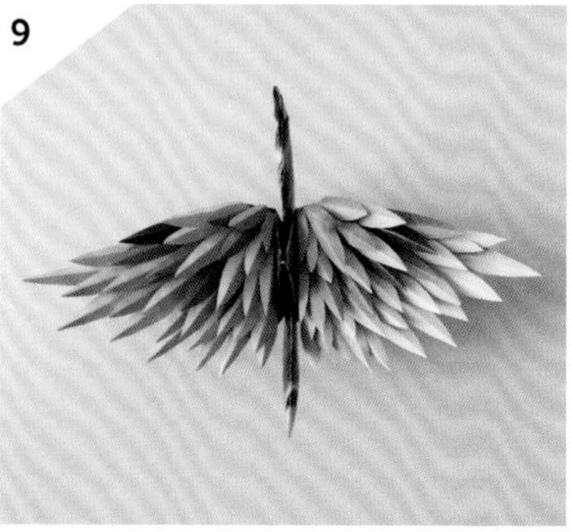

10

11a

11b

11c

TANT CRANE

This striking variation is made from tant paper – colourful origami paper with a crêpe paper feel – plus leftover magazine and coloured paper.

MATERIALS

- 1 sheet of 15 x 15 cm tant paper for the crane
- Coloured paper (optional)
- Magazine paper (optional)
- Clear glue
- Scissors
- Bamboo stick

PATTERNS

- Approximately ten of each Type A feather: A1, A2, A3, A4, A5, A6, A7, A8 and A9 (see page 157)

DIFFICULTY ✳✳

INSTRUCTIONS

Fold a Basic Crane (see page 82). Use the same technique as in the previous three crane designs to attach the feathers, using as many feathers as you desire to fill your design. The photos show the arrangement of feathers and the result when smaller feathers are used.

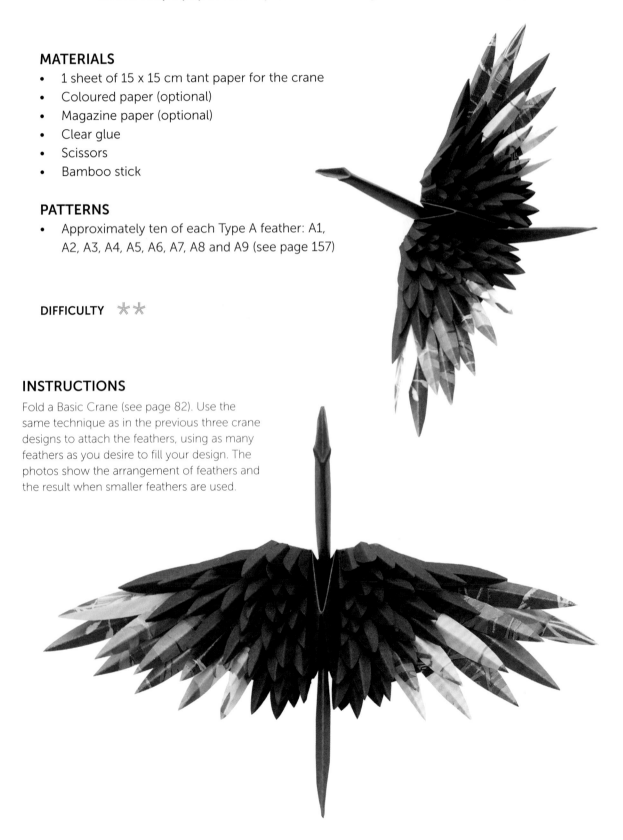

ROMANTIC ROSE

What could be more romantic on Valentine's Day than a single
stem rose, especially one you have made yourself?

MATERIALS

- 2 sheets of A4 100–120 gsm paper for the rose petals
- 1.25 mm florist wire for the stem, approximately 37 cm in length
- 0.5 mm florist wire to attach the leaves
- Florist tape in moss green
- 5 x 10 cm piece of tissue paper or mulberry paper
- Clear glue   •   Scissors   •   Bamboo stick

PATTERNS

- 3 x each of the Petals: P1, P2, P3, P4, P5 and P6 and
  2 x Leaves: L1 (see page 156)

DIFFICULTY ✴✴✴

TIP

Don't worry if the wire for the
stem is bumpy as you can
wrap another layer of tape
around it at the end.

INSTRUCTIONS

Forming the Stem

1 Attach a couple of lengths of
0.5 mm florist wire to the 1.25 mm
wire stem, trim to your desired size
and wrap with florist tape. For extra
security, add a small amount of
glue at the beginning and at the
end of the tape. You can repeat
this process a couple of times.

2 Layer a narrow layer of green
tissue paper or mulberry paper on
top of a wider white strip and roll
up to make the pistil. The double-
layered side will be the top – make
sure this is thickest part. The single
layered bottom part is easy to
attach to the stem.

3 Stick the stem into the thinner
end of the pistil and secure with
florist tape.

Making the Petals

1 Cut out 3 x petals from each
size. Cut out a small triangle from
the bottom of each petal.

2 Curve one side of the top of
each petal using the bamboo stick.

3 Apply glue at the bottom of each
petal (up to the pencil line shown
in the photograph), above the
cut-out triangle.

4 Use the triangle at the bottom
to create a curved shape when
attaching the petals and keep a
space between them. Place the
next petal overlapping about
one-third to half of the previous
petal at the base of the flower.

5 Wait for the glue to dry before
adding another petal. Start from
the smallest petal, and use about
three or four petals of each size.

6 Add more petals until you reach
your desired flower size.

Attaching the Leaves

1 Cut out 2 x leaves. Fold each leaf
in the middle.

2 Glue the thin wire to the back of
each leaf to secure.

3 Your Romantic Rose is now
finished!

Stem

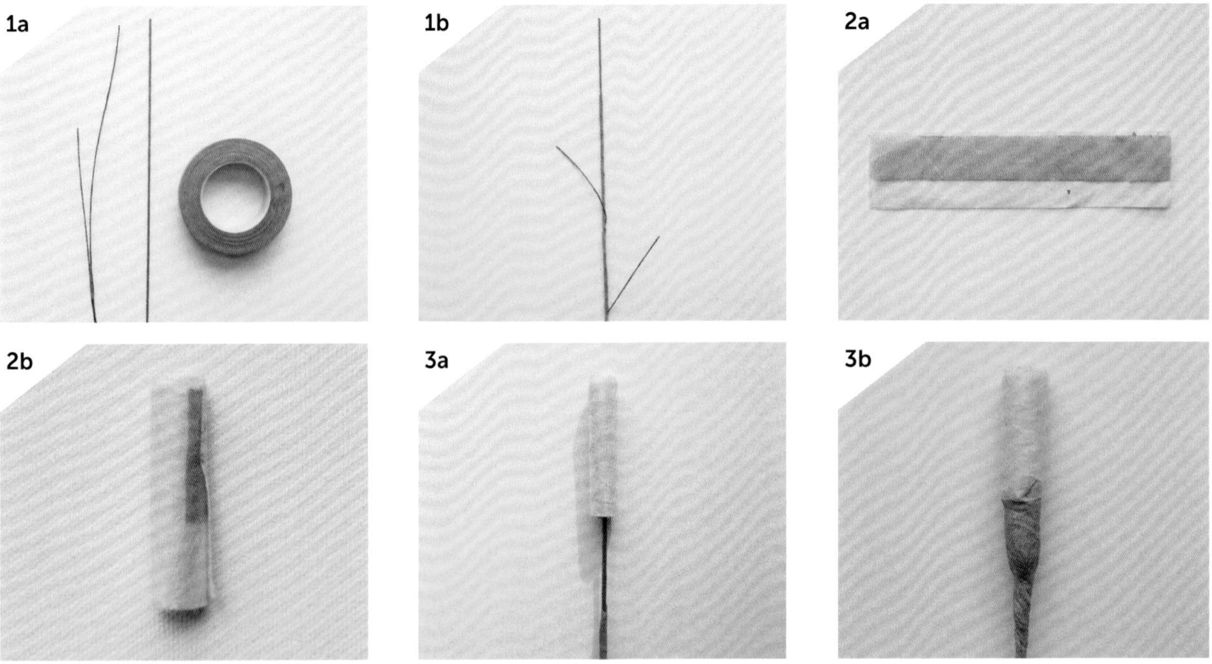

1a

1b

2a

2b

3a

3b

Petals

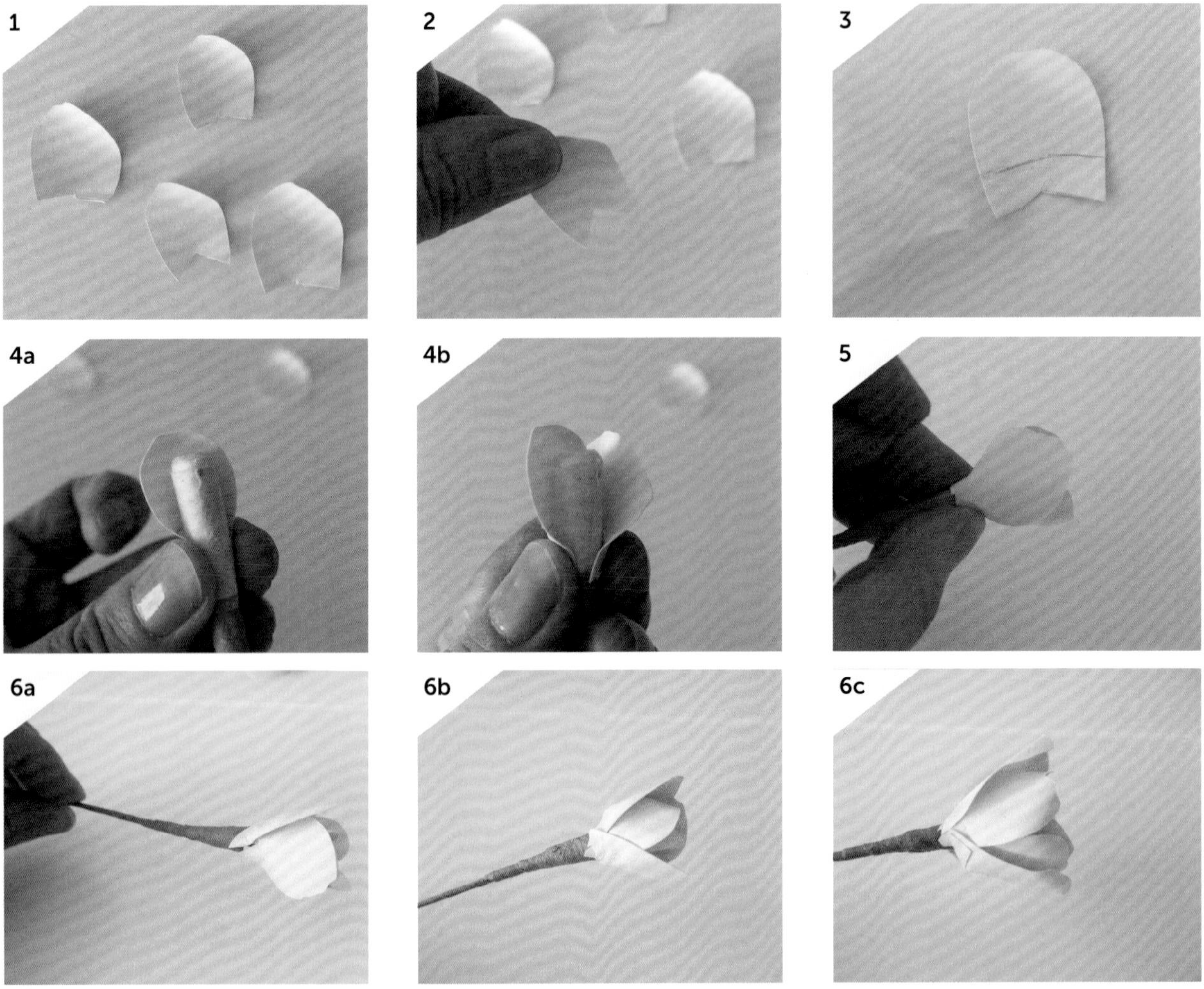

1

2

3

4a

4b

5

6a

6b

6c

6d

6e

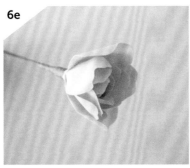

6f

6g

6h

6i

Leaves

1

2

3

PROUD PARROT

The parrot's colourful patterned wings give this traditional origami design a modern eye-catching touch.

MATERIALS

- 1 sheet of 15 x 15 cm tant paper for the body
- 2 sheets of 9 x 9 cm Yuzen washi paper for the wings
- Scissors
- Clear glue

DIFFICULTY ★★★★★

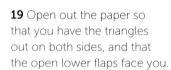

INSTRUCTIONS

Head and Body

1 Fold along both diagonals and unfold.

2 Bring the two corners towards the centre line.

3 Turn the paper over and rotate 45 degrees anticlockwise. Bring the top half to the bottom point.

4 Turn the paper over. Lift up the top right flap and following the flap's crease line, bring that side to the centre line.

5 Repeat step 4 on the other side. Your paper will look like this.

6 Bring the behind flap up.

7 Fold the central triangle so it faces the bottom tip.

8 Fold the inside corners in half, towards the outside edge.

9 Fold the flaps in half again from the outside edge towards the central horizontal line.

10 Unfold steps 8–9.

11 On the right-hand triangle, fold the right edge upwards along your valley crease to the central horizontal line, then pinch the pointed paper facing you. Bring this over to the right side and flatten. You will have a small triangle now.

12 Repeat step 11 on the other side.

13 Folding along the centre, bring the left half onto the right half.

14 Fold the right-hand side back over to the outer edge.

15 Fold the other flap behind. The small triangles should stick out.

16 Folding at the lower $^1/_6$, bring the top half down. The point will be level with the triangles.

17 Finding halfway between the fold line and top of the paper behind, as shown, fold the flap back up.

18 Unfold steps 16–17.

19 Open out the paper so that you have the triangles out on both sides, and that the open lower flaps face you.

20 Mountain and valley fold along the two top creases.

21 Mountain fold the centre line.

22 Fold and unfold the tip of your paper at an angle.

23 Inside reverse fold along the creases to make the parrot's face.

24 Fold the tip of the face up at an angle and unfold.

25 Inside reverse fold on the tip of the beak.

26 Outside reverse fold the very tip of the beak.

27 Fold the front flap in half to the centre line.

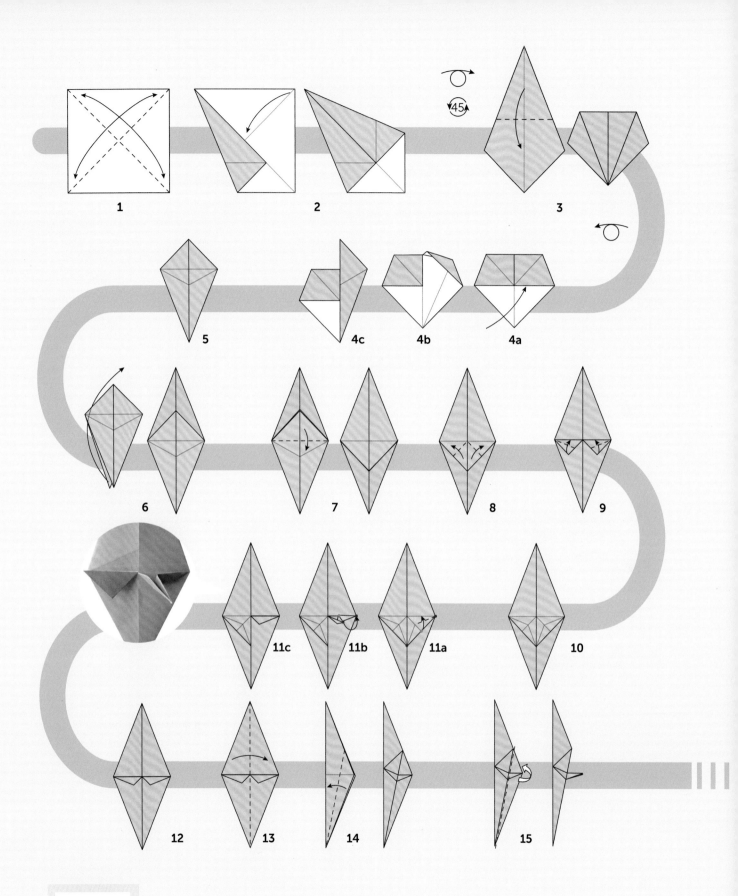

1

2

3

5 4c 4b 4a

6 7 8 9

11c 11b 11a 10

12 13 14 15

Scan for a tutorial!

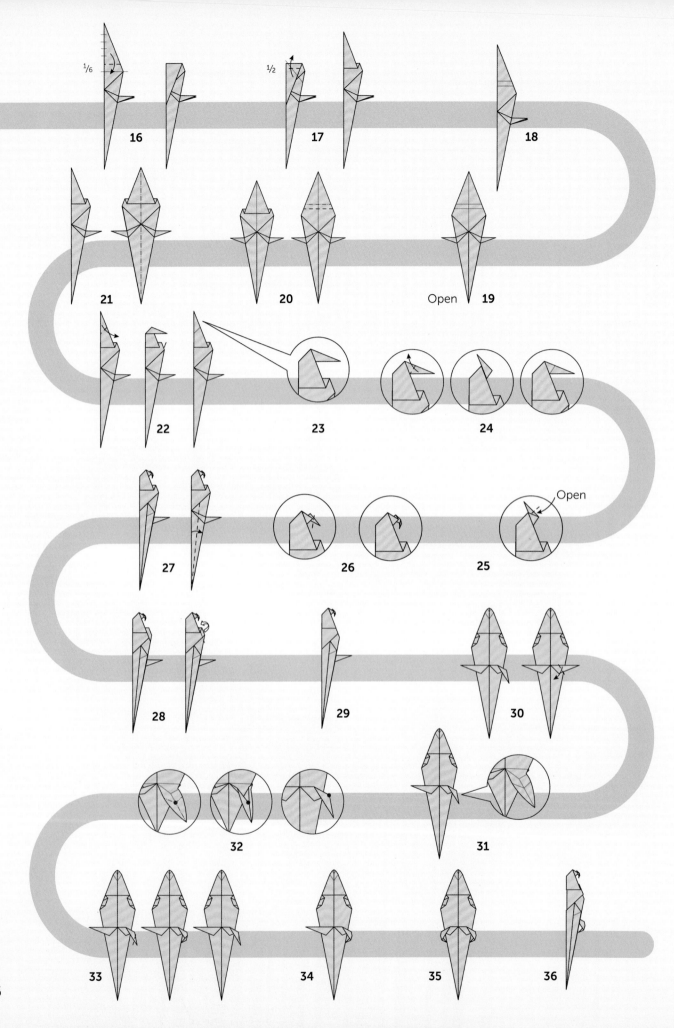

28 Mountain fold the paper just under the neck backwards to the body.

29 Flip the paper and repeat steps 27–28 on the other side. This will lengthen the parrot's neck.

30 Open up your paper in half. Fold down one of the triangles at an angle to make the feet.

31 Unfold step 30 and open the flap.

32 Outside reverse fold: mountain fold following the creases.

33 Fold the tip in towards the centre line and unfold.

34 Inside reverse fold the tip of the foot using the crease lines.

35 Repeat steps 30–34 on the other side.

36 Your parrot's body is complete!

Wings

1 Fold in half and unfold.

2 Fold the top in half to make ¼, then unfold. Turn the paper over.

3 Bring the top half of your paper down, making a mountain fold between your crease lines, so that the ¼ crease line matches the half-line behind. This has now made an $\frac{1}{8}$.

4 Bring the top half of the paper down again, making a mountain fold, so that your ¼ crease line matches your $\frac{1}{8}$ line. This has now made a $\frac{1}{16}$.

5 Turn the paper 90 degrees clockwise. Bring the bottom edge up in half to the top edge.

6 On the top layer of your paper, fold the top half of the flap down.

7 Repeat step 6 on the flap behind then unfold your paper completely.

8 Bring the bottom edge up to ¼ line.

9 Continue to pleat fold to the centre following the mountain fold line on ¼ line, then valley fold up to the centre line.

10 Repeat steps 8–9 on the top half and unfold everything. Your paper will now be in $\frac{1}{8}$ segments.

11 Turn the paper over and fold the bottom edge up to the first $\frac{1}{8}$ crease line.

12 Continue to pleat fold to the centre, following mountain and valley creases.

13 Continue steps 11–12 on the top half from the centre line and unfold everything. Your paper will now be in $\frac{1}{16}$ segments.

14 Fold the bottom edge up to the first $\frac{1}{16}$ crease line.

15 Continue and pleat fold to the centre. You may find it easier to unfold your paper as you go, or to keep it in a folded clump.

16 Continue steps 14–15 on the top half and unfold everything. Your paper will now be in $\frac{1}{32}$ segments.

17 Fold the bottom and top $\frac{1}{32}$ to the next crease line, then turn your paper over.

18 Pleat fold on the right-hand side, follow the first crease as a mountain fold and the second crease as a valley fold.

19 Mountain fold on the second crease from the bottom so that your paper is behind.

20 Valley fold the next crease line.

21 Leaving a gap of a crease, mountain fold the next crease line line, skip a crease then valley fold the next one.

22 Repeat the corrugation until the end – you might find it helpful to use a paperclip to hold the ones you have done. You should have 7 in total.

23 Turn the paper anticlockwise 90 degrees. Mountain fold the top flap behind.

24 Mountain fold the last three on the left-hand side.

25 Use a mountain fold to tuck the top edge behind.

26 For the left side wing, fold the bottom left diagonal behind.

27 Cut the extra part and hide the fold behind.

28 The left wing is complete. Repeat the wing steps with opposite fold directions for the right wing.

29 Glue the wings to the sides and your Parrot is complete!

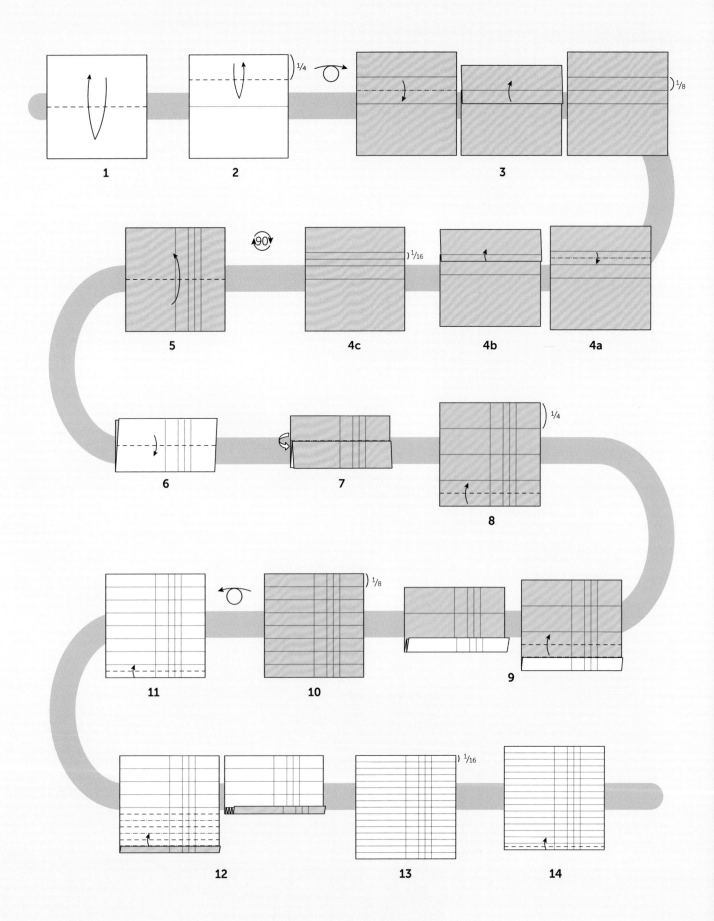

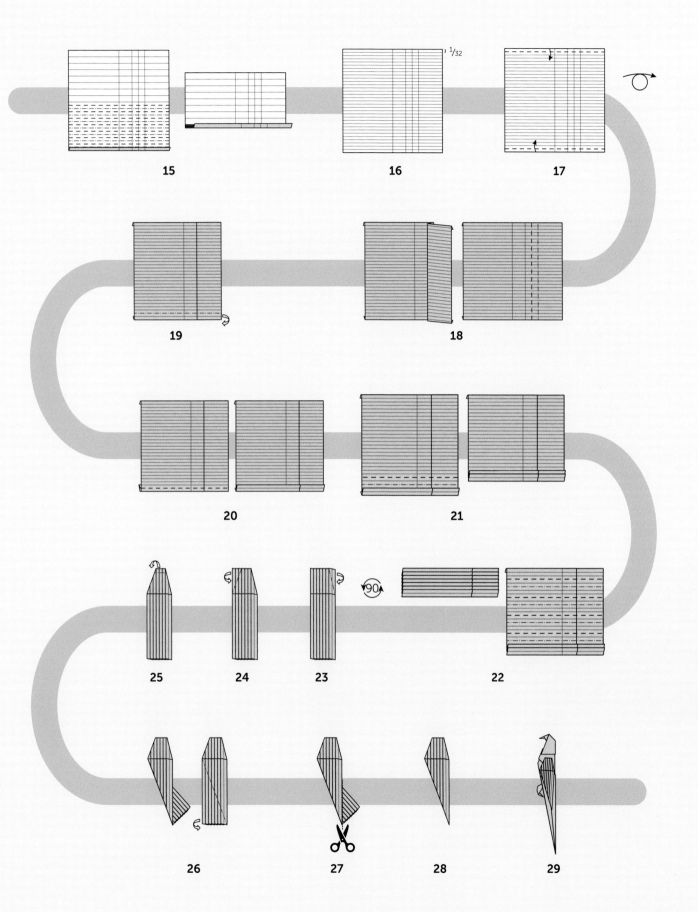

15

16

$^1/_{32}$

17

19

18

20

21

25

24

23

90

22

26

27

28

29

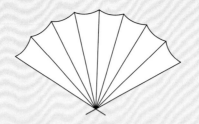

GIFT WRAPPING

Introduction

Wrapping plays an important role in Japanese culture and some key Japanese wrapping styles are practised and explored in this chapter. The style of gift wrap used can reveal a lot about the relationship between the gift giver and recipient; it can even reflect the seasons. Sending a gift is like wrapping the heart – the gift should be wrapped delicately and carefully – the beauty is in the gentleness.

Your choice of paper and wrapping style will depend on who you are sending the gift to. You don't have to use luxury paper, but the correct choice of colour and style are more important. 'The thicker, the better' is not true for wrapping paper. Thick paper can be hard to fold and is sometimes very brittle; strong, thin paper is a better choice. Soft but tough paper such as Yuzen washi, which is used on several samples in this chapter, is also ideal for gift wrapping.

As well as paper choice, you will also need to consider how best to decorate your box. A range of decorations are included at the end of the chapter that will give an extra-special finishing touch to show how much you care. Discover how to make a paper fan, leaf, rose or crane to attach to your gift box, in addition to a simple ribbon bow, ribbon knot or string flower to complete the look – and they are all easier to make than you'd imagine. You can even recycle leftover gift wrap, combining it to form a unique collage effect.

To get a neat seam, double-sided tape is best. Ribbon is not a must-have – instead, you can use paper strips to make banners and bows, which may require some practice at the beginning. Start with the basic wrap and then add some additions to the paper such as pleat folds. When you can master the basic wrapping techniques with different types of paper, try the kimono style for a truly professional look.

BASIC WRAPPING

For the neatest edges, it is worth mastering this basic wrapping style, which you can then adorn in any way you please.

MATERIALS
- 1 sheet of wrapping paper
- Double-sided tape

DIFFICULTY ✳

INSTRUCTIONS

1 Cut the wrapping paper to size. It should be long enough to cover one round of the box, plus 1 cm for tape; the width should the width of the box plus two-thirds of the thickness of the box at top and bottom.

2 Bring the two sides to the middle and fix with double-sided tape.

3 Fold the top and bottom of the taped side close to the box to fold the corners.

4 On one flap, fold the two outer corners in towards the box.

5 Fold this flap up against the box.

6 Fold back the outer edge in line with where it meets the side folds, then unfold.

7 Inside reverse fold the edge and fix with double-sided tape. Repeat steps 4–7 on the other flap.

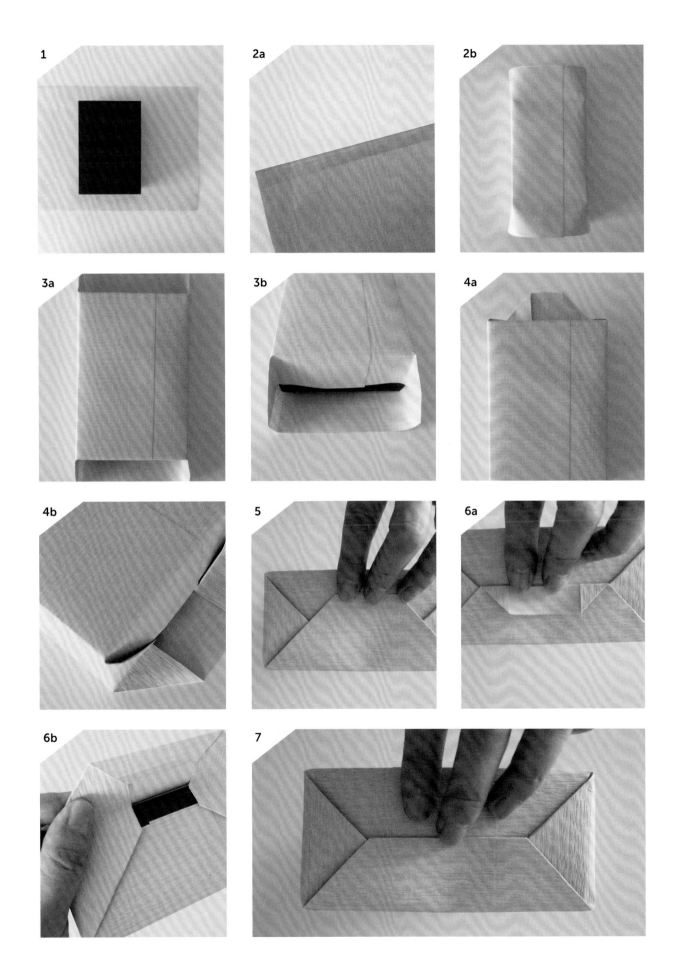

PLEAT FOLD WRAPPING

The neat pleats on top give any gift a stylish edge,
topped with a simple bow for a final flourish.

MATERIALS

- 1 sheet of wrapping paper
- Double-sided tape
- Sellotape
- Ribbon

DIFFICULTY ✳✳

INSTRUCTIONS

1 Cut the wrapping paper to size. It should be long enough to cover one round of the box plus the width of the box (to make pleats), with an extra 1 cm for tape. The width should be the width of the box plus two-thirds of the thickness of the box at top and bottom.

2 Take the width of the box from the middle of the wrapping paper and pleat fold in your desired number of pleats.

3 Unfold the paper.

4 Collapse the pleats.

5 Flip over and tape from inside, near the top, middle and bottom, to fix the pleats.

6 Follow steps 2–7 of Basic Wrapping (see page 102) to wrap the box in the basic style.

7 Cut the ribbon long enough to wrap the box horizontally, plus 20 cm

for the bow. Place the box in the centre of the ribbon and make a fold on the right end of the ribbon, making sure the fold reaches the left edge of the box.

8 Bring the left side of the ribbon on top of the right end.

9 Fold the left end behind, underneath all the ribbon layers.

10 Bring the left end up.

11 Tuck the left end behind the first layer of ribbon from the left. Gently stretch the right side fold and left side end to tighten the knot.

12 Place double-sided tape behind the knot to seal the ribbon to the box. Trim the length of the ribbon to your desired length to finish.

TIP

Add a decoration for an extra flourish (see pages 119–124), or keep it simple with thin string in a contrasting colour over the ribbon!

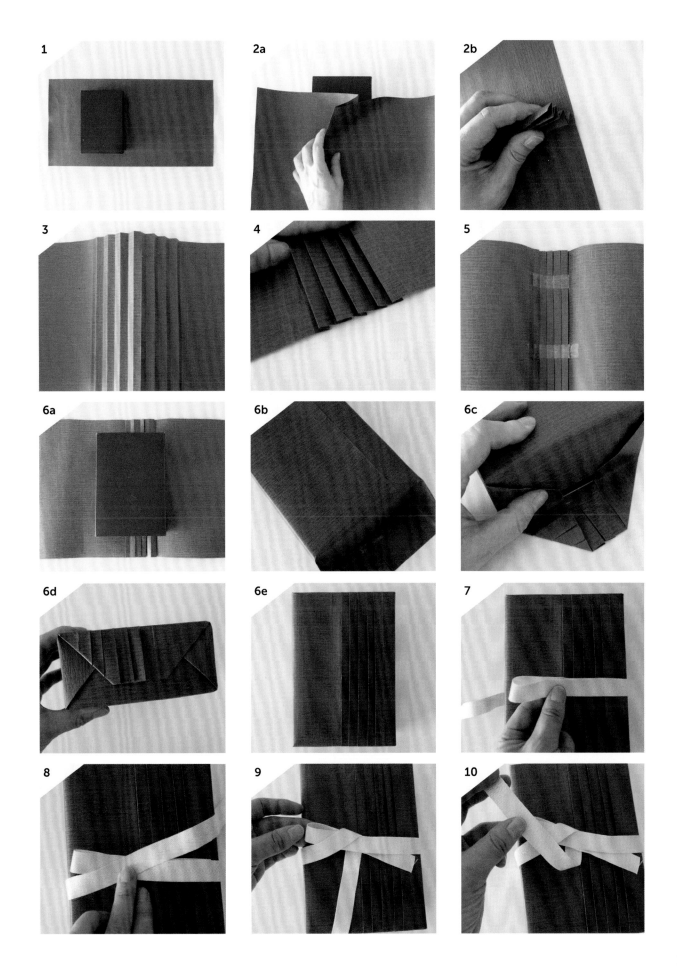

KIMONO-STYLE WRAPPING

For the ultimate in wrapping style, this kimono-style wrap looks so professional finished with a complementary banner and intricate paper tassel.

MATERIALS
- 1 sheet of wrapping paper
- 1 sheet of paper for the banner
- 2 pieces of 4.5 x 9 cm Yuzen washi paper (or other suitable paper) for the tassels
- Ribbon (optional) • String for the tassel
- Double-sided tape

DIFFICULTY ✳✳

INSTRUCTIONS

1 Cut the wrapping paper to size. The length of the paper should cover the box vertically; the width should cover the box horizontally (one round) plus the width of the box.

2 Bring the top part down to the bottom edge of the box. Firmly crease along the top edge.

3 Firmly crease the side edges.

4 Open the left-hand side up and bring the top edge's crease down to the side of the box, to create a pair of triangular flaps.

5 Bring the front triangular flap over your box and flatten. The bottom edges of your paper should line up.

6 Repeat steps 4–5 on the right-hand side of your paper. Fix the left corner of this layer to the side of your box with double-sided tape.

7 Your wrapped box will look like this.

8 Fold the outer left and right flaps across the box, as in step 5.

9 Fix the top flap's bottom left corner in place with double-sided tape.

10 Close the bottom of the box in the same way as in Basic Wrapping (see page 102), and secure with double-sided tape.

11 Your wrapped box should look like this.

12 Wrap a banner around the bottom half of the kimono and secure it in place with double-sided tape. Finish by tying a ribbon around the banner and adding a tassel, as desired.

TIP
The banner shown here is pleat folded, but you can choose any style you like to complete the look. It could also be double layered or folded.

ORIGAMI AND KIRIGAMI FOR THE HOME

9b

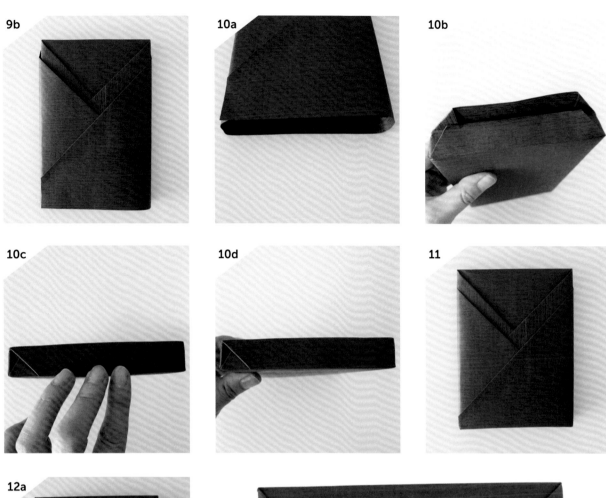

10a

10b

10c

10d

11

12a

12b

Tassel

1 Take your string and a 4.5 x 9 cm piece of paper.

2 Fold the paper in half.

3 Cut slits along the open side of the paper, making the cuts an even length and consistently spaced.

4 Make your cuts as fine as possible.

5 Apply glue on the uncut closed side.

6 Place one end of your string onto the glued paper.

7 Roll the paper onto the string.

8 Hold the rolled paper in position until the glue is dry to stop it from opening.

9 Repeat to make a second tassel on the other side of the string and tie around the banner of your gift-wrapped box.

Kimono Variation

For a different look, fold the left-hand flaps to the front and the right-hand flaps to the back of your gift, then tuck a gift card in the overlap.

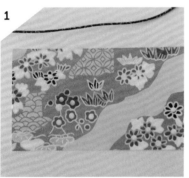

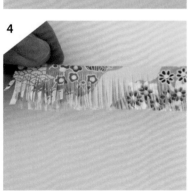

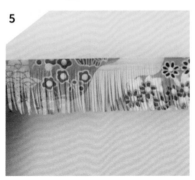

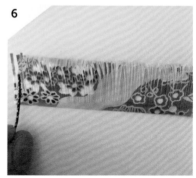

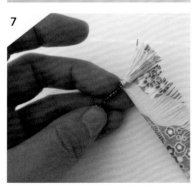

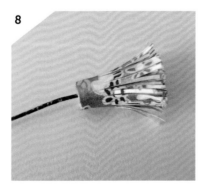

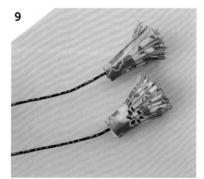

POCKET WRAPPING

For a clever twist, tuck a gift card into the pocket at the front of this gorgeously wrapped gift.

MATERIALS
- 1 sheet of wrapping paper
- Double-sided tape

DIFFICULTY ✶✶

INSTRUCTIONS

Size Your wrapping paper should be long enough to wrap around the box once; the width should cover the box plus two-thirds of the thickness of the box at top and bottom. If the box is too thin, leave more paper and fold it behind.

1 Wrap the right-hand side of your paper across the front of the box to cover it. Fold down the top left corner on the left-hand side.

2 Bring the folded left side to the right-hand side and fix in place with double-sided tape.

3 Close the top and bottom in the same way as in Basic Wrapping (see page 102).

4 When closing, if you have extra paper, fold the bottom flap up and bring down together with the upper flap. Secure in place at the back with double-sided tape.

5 Your finished pocket wrapped gift should look like this. Don't forget to add a gift card to the pocket!

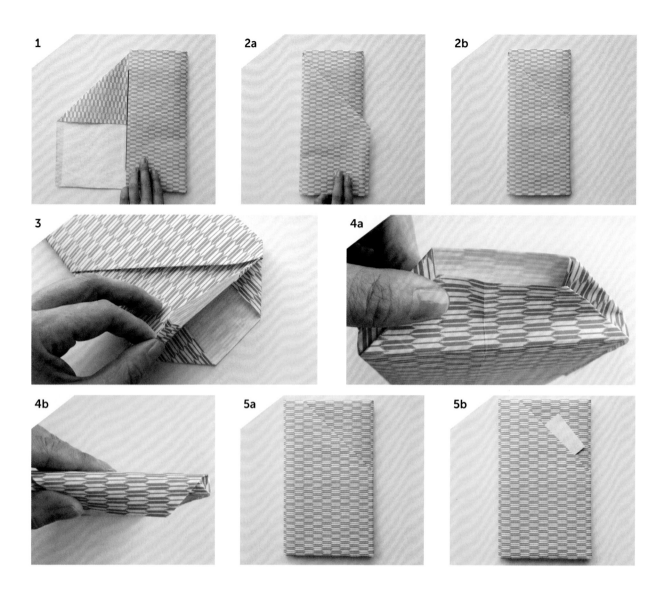

SUIT-STYLE WRAPPING

What better way to wrap a present for that special man in your life than with this smart tuxedo and bow tie style?

MATERIALS

- 1 sheet of textured paper (for the tuxedo)
- 1 sheet of textured paper (for the shirt)
- 1 sheet of printed origami paper (for the bow tie)
- Clear tape
- Double-sided tape

DIFFICULTY ✳✳✳

INSTRUCTIONS

Shirt

1 The width of the paper for the shirt should be one round of the box plus 7 cm (1 cm for the tape and 6 cm for the centre pleats). The length of the paper should be the length of box plus two-thirds of the thickness of the box at the top and bottom.

2 Fold the paper horizontally in half.

3 Pleat fold the middle section by bringing the left side over then folding it back on itself.

4 Collapse the pleat fold and follow the creases to make a raised strip of paper in the centre.

5 Flip the paper over and use clear tape to fix the folds on this side, then place your box in the middle of the paper.

6 Wrap the box following the instructions for Basic Wrapping (see page 102). Make sure the pleat-folded section stays in the centre.

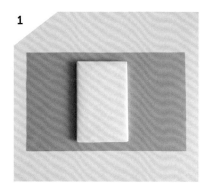

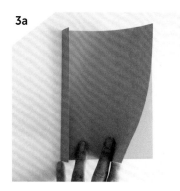

4a

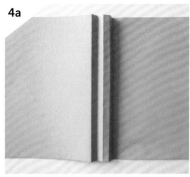

4b

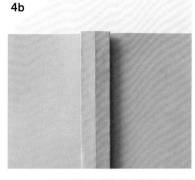

5

6

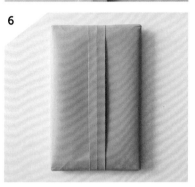

Tuxedo

1 The paper for the suit should be the same width as the box and long enough to wrap across the box.

2 Fold in the two upper corners at an angle to make the collar. Bring across the box then fix in place at the centre with double-sided tape.

Bow Tie

1 For the tie you will need a 10 x 10 cm of paper to give an 11-cm-wide tie.

2 Fold across both diagonals and unfold.

3 Fold the top and bottom corners to the centre point.

4 Bring the top and bottom edges to the centre line.

5 Fold in half, bringing the left side on top of the right side.

6 On the closed edge, fold in the two corners to the centre line.

7 Unfold and inside reverse fold the corners.

1

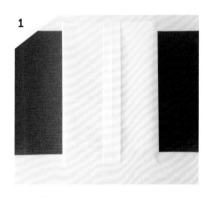

2

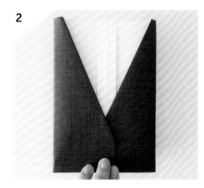

8 Bring the front flap up, then bring the back flap up behind it.

9 Turn your paper 180 degrees. Fold both corners in to the centre line, then repeat on the flap behind.

10 Carefully pull open the flaps and flatten the middle square.

11 Your bow tie is now finished!

12 For a different style of bow tie, simply fold the corners behind.

1

2

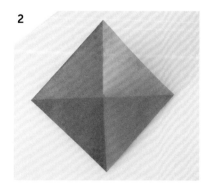

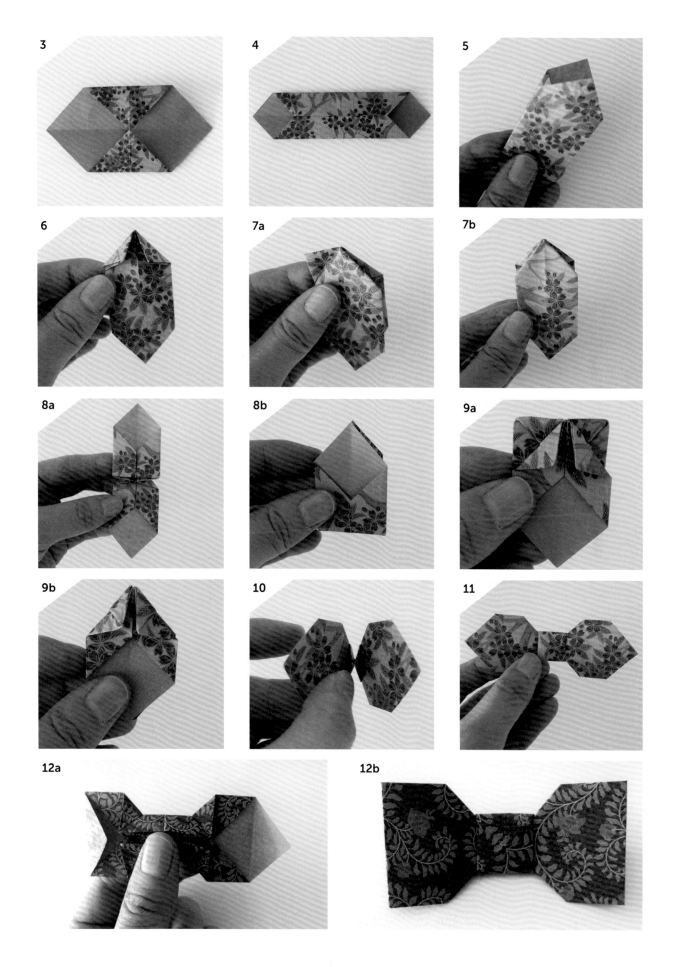

WINE GIFT BAG

A bottle of wine makes a lovely gift, and it's even better when presented in a homemade gift bag. The card paper adds strength to the bag.

MATERIALS

- 1 sheet of 45 x 45 cm strong wrapping paper
- A 10 x 10 cm card paper square
- 2 card paper strips measuring 3 x 10 cm
- Ribbon or string (60 cm in length or longer)
- Clear glue
- Hole punch/awl

DIFFICULTY ✳✳✳

INSTRUCTIONS

1 Make 4 x 10 cm and 1 x 5 cm wide pleat folds in the strong wrapping paper, following step 2 of Pleat Fold Wrapping (see page 104).

2 Apply glue across the 5-cm wide strip on the patterned side.

3 Bring the other end of your paper to the glued end to make a cuboid tube.

4 When the glue has dried completely, flatten the bag. Fold 3 cm down from the top edge then fold the same again. Unfold.

5 Fold the bottom edge up 6 cm and unfold.

6 On the bottom edge, fold both corners up to the crease line and unfold. Repeat on the reverse side.

7 Open the bag into a cuboid tube. Follow the creases made in step 6 to fold the bottom of the bag: bring the sides in to the centre and then fold the pointed flaps on top.

8 Glue the flaps down on the bottom and leave to dry.

9 Glue the 10 x 10 cm card paper inside to the base of the bag.

10 Glue the two 3 x 10 cm card strips onto the inside top edge of the bag, opposite to each other.

11 Using the crease lines from step 4, fold all four top edges down to wrap the card strips. Repeat the fold.

12 Use the hole punch or awl to punch holes at the top into the two sides with card inside. Thread the ribbon or string through all four holes and tie with a knot inside.

13 Your Wine Gift Bag is now complete!

1a

1b

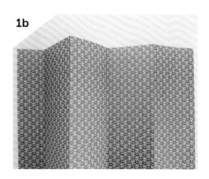

2

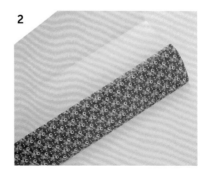

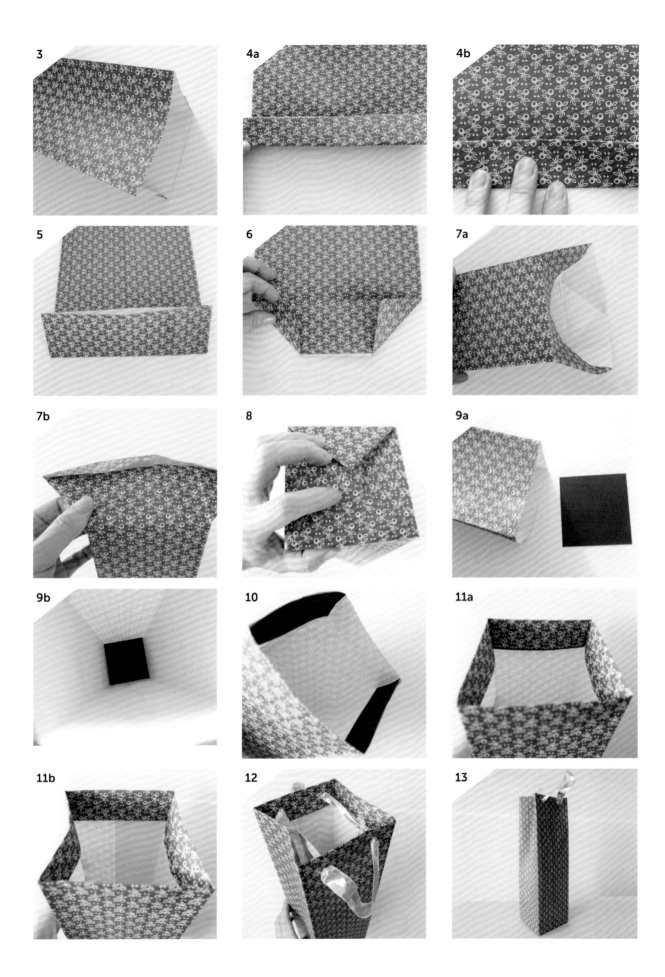

RIBBONS AND DECORATIONS

These simple accessories will complement your wrapping style
to give your gifts an impressive finishing touch.

FAN

This fan can be made in a flash with some simple pleat folds and washi tape.

MATERIALS

- 7 x 7 cm any suitable paper
  (or size to fit your gift box)
- Washi tape

DIFFICULTY ✳

INSTRUCTIONS

1 Pleat fold from side to side.

2 Pinch together at one side to
form a fan shape.

3 Wrap washi tape around the base
of the fan to join the fold together.

1

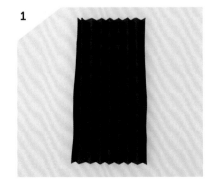

2

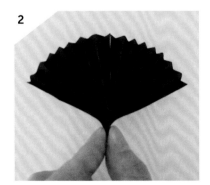

3

LEAF

This lovely leaf would make a great addition to an autumn birthday gift.

MATERIALS

- 10 x 10 cm any suitable paper (or size to fit your gift box)
- Washi tape

DIFFICULTY ✳

INSTRUCTIONS

1 Pleat fold the paper diagonally from one corner to another.

2 Pinch the bottom part of the folds together between your fingers.

3 Fold all the layers in half in the bottom half to form the stem.

4 Fix in place with washi tape.

5 Your leaf is now finished.

ROSE

The size of this rose decoration can be altered by varying the number of petals.

MATERIALS

- 1 sheet of 110gsm paper to suit your gift box (A4 or size to fit your gift box)
- Pen
- Scissors
- Wooden pegs
- Clear glue
- Wooden skewers

PATTERNS

- Petals: P1, P2, P3, P4, P5, P6 (see page 156)
- Leaves: L1, L2, L3 (see page 156)

DIFFICULTY ✳✳✳

INSTRUCTIONS

1 Follow the instructions to make a rose from the Rose Wall Panel (see page 62), this time using fewer petals to make a smaller flower of a suitable size for your gift box.

MINIATURE CRANE

Add a special touch to your gift with this little symbol of good luck.

MATERIALS

- 7 x 7 cm paper (or size to fit your gift box)

DIFFICULTY ✳✳✳

INSTRUCTIONS

1 Follow the instructions for the Basic Crane (see page 82), omitting steps 7, 8 and 9, so the neck and tail are not as thin.

2 Fold the front wing down at any desired angle.

SIMPLE RIBBON BOW

A simple but stunning way to add a bow to finish off your beautiful wrapping.

MATERIALS
- Ribbon
- Double-sided tape

DIFFICULTY ✳

INSTRUCTIONS

1 Use a small piece of ribbon to make a ring. Fix in place with double-sided tape.

2 Repeat step 1 with a longer piece of ribbon to make a slightly bigger ring.

3 Secure the smaller ring on top of the larger ring using double-sided tape to complete the bow.

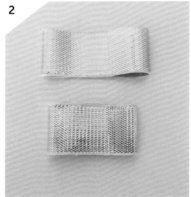

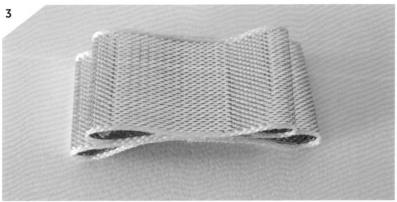

RIBBON KNOT

Commonly used for weddings, funerals and get well wishes, the knot can symbolise stable relationships and feelings of condolence.

MATERIALS

- 15 x 1.5 cm ribbon
- Double-sided tape

DIFFICULTY ✳

INSTRUCTIONS

1 If you are using a wider ribbon, the length should be ten times the width to form your knot.

2 Bring the right side end up to the front. Leave a longer length of ribbon to the left.

3 Bring the left side end up on top of the right side.

4 Fold the left side behind the right side.

5 Gently tighten the knot.

6 Attach it to your gift box at any preferred angle using double-sided tape.

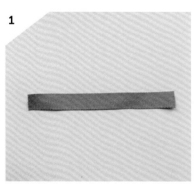

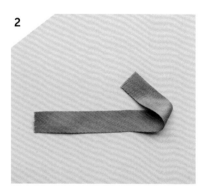

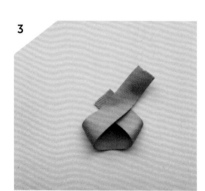

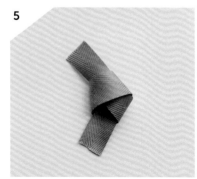

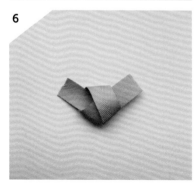

STRING FLOWER

So simple and elegant, this string flower
adds an instant touch of class.

MATERIALS

- 37 cm length of decorative string
- Cotton or any thin thread

DIFFICULTY ✱✱

INSTRUCTIONS

Size The length of your decorative string should be the width of your desired flower plus 1 cm.

1 Start from one end and fold back about 3 cm (half of the width of the flower).

2 Continue to wave the string and gather in the centre.

3 The overall shape should look like this.

4 Use a short length of cotton (or any thin thread) to tie the petals together at the centre. Tie twice to make sure it is fixed securely.

5 Trim off the thread's ends and adjust the shape to finish.

1
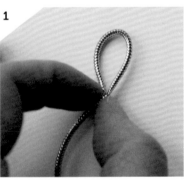

2a
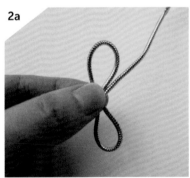

2b

2c

3

4

5
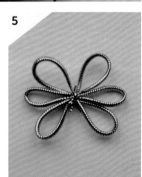

COLLAGE GIFT WRAP

Give used gift wrap a new lease of life by combining two pieces of leftover paper in any style to beautifully wrap another present.

MATERIALS

- Two pieces of wrapping paper
- Clear or tacky glue or double-sided tape

DIFFICULTY

INSTRUCTIONS

1 Cut your two pieces of wrapping paper to the same length.

2 Fold up 1 cm on the patterned side of the first piece of paper and 1 cm on the plain side of the second piece.

3 Apply glue or double-sided tape to the plain strip of the paper.

4 Connect the two pieces sticking the folded flaps together, as shown.

5 Your Collage Gift Wrap is now ready to use. Wrap your box following the instructions for Basic Wrapping (see page 102).

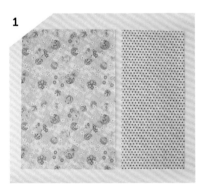

1

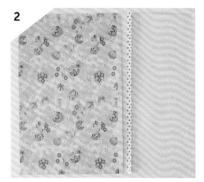

2

3

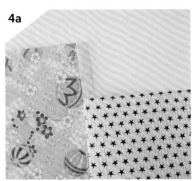

4a

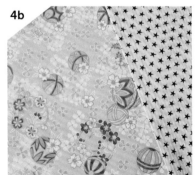

4b

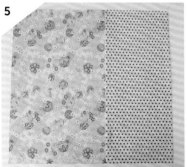

5

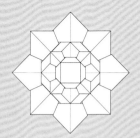

GREETING CARDS

Introduction

A handcrafted greeting card is a gift in itself. The effort that is put into crafting a homemade gift card that is unique to the recipient makes it something to be displayed with pride and treasured for years to come.

The first card design features an ornate origami Kaleidoscope Flower (see page 128), which looks stunning simply adorning a plain coloured card on its own. Tant paper is ideal for this design, as the colours and shades available perfectly complement the kaleidoscope theme. The flowers can also be presented in a pair, using pastel-toned printed origami paper, with their stems and leaves simply drawn in with colouring pencil for a no-fuss finishing touch.

The idea of making two or more traditional origami plates in contrasting tones and arranging them together to form a multicoloured pattern is inspired by the kaleidoscope. A simple yet elegant design, the colours of the flower can be tailored to suit the occasion. Make it in pastel shades to welcome a new addition to the family, or use festive colours such as red, gold and green for a poinsettia-inspired Christmas card.

Dollmaking is rich in Japanese character and tradition. The second card in this chapter, the kimono-clad paper doll (*Anesama Ningyō*), is a design that has been favoured by young girls in Japan since the Edo period. Here it has been adapted into a simple, flat version that will brighten up any greeting (see page 130).

Washi and chiyogami papers are usually used in dolls clothing, and textured washi that comes in plain colours is used for special occasions. The colour of the doll's kimono can be changed to reflect the season, the event or even the tastes and style of the recipient, making it really special and full of character.

For a simple winter greeting, the final card design is always a crowd-pleaser. This snowflake comprises two copies of the design, so experimenting with a silver paper and a light blue, or a less traditional mix of colours, will look gorgeous on any festive card. For a flurry, use smaller-sized paper to make mini snowflakes on a card or around the home.

KALEIDOSCOPE FLOWER

This traditional design is simple to fold but looks so effective when made up in bold contrasting colours, chosen to suit the occasion.

MATERIALS

- 2 sheets of 7 x 7 cm tant or printed origami paper
- 2 sheets of 3.5 x 3.5 cm tant or printed origami paper (a quarter of the size)
- Scissors or a craft knife   • Clear glue

DIFFICULTY ✳✳

INSTRUCTIONS

1 Fold in half and unfold.

2 Fold the top and bottom edges up to the centre line and unfold.

3 Turn 90 degrees anticlockwise and repeat steps 1–2.

4 Bring each corner to the centre point and unfold.

5 Turn the paper over. Follow the existing creases and bring the marked points towards the centre. It should look like 5c. Squash down the top flaps.

6 On each square, fold the centre corner of the flap to the outside corner.

7 On the top right square, bring the left side onto the right.

8 Fold the top layer of this flap back on itself to the centre line.

9 Bring the folded flap back to the left side. Repeat steps 7–9 on all remaining flaps.

10 Your paper should look like this!

11 Follow steps 1–10 to make another model of the same size.

12 Cut one of the models into four pieces, cutting along the straight lines to the centre. This one will be cut into the accented pieces.

13 Insert the cut pieces into your second main model.

14 Folding up from the centre point on the top-left flap to the top-right flap, make a triangle.

15 Tuck the tip of the triangle into the accented piece to secure the flap.

16 Repeat steps 13–15 with each cut piece.

17 Using your two smaller pieces of paper, follow steps 1–16 to make a smaller flower decoration.

18 Glue the smaller flower onto the gap in the centre of the larger one. Your Kaleidoscope Flower is now complete!

TIP

To make a triple flower, use 2 sheets of 15 x 15 cm tant paper for the biggest flower, 2 sheets of 7.5 x 7.5 cm tant paper for the middle flower, and 2 sheets of 3.75 x 3.75 cm tant paper for the smallest flower!

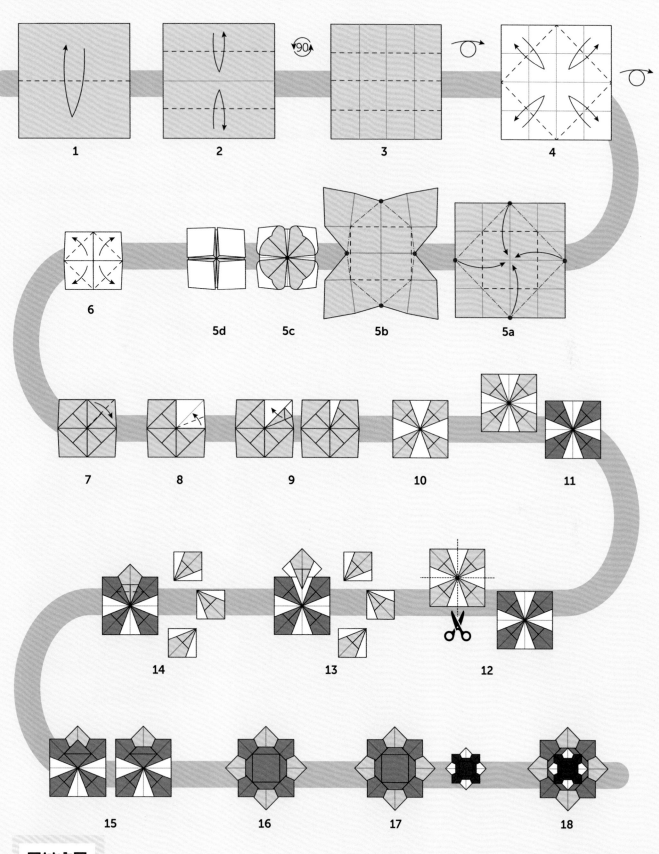

1

2

3

4

5a

5b

5c

5d

6

7

8

9

10

11

12

13

14

15

16

17

18

Scan for a tutorial!

PAPER DOLL IN KIMONO

This traditional kimono-clad doll has been inspired by *Anesama Ningyō*, meaning 'big sister dolls'. They are known for their elaborate hairstyles and lack of facial features.

MATERIALS

- 1 sheet of A5 card paper for making the templates
- 1 sheet of 3 x 3 cm 150 gsm white paper for the head
- 1 sheet of 3 x 3 cm 150 gsm black paper for the hair
- 1 sheet of 9 x 9 cm patterned chiyogami paper for the first layer
- 2 sheets of 3.5 x 7 cm patterned chiyogami paper for the second layer
- 2 sheets of 6 x 12 cm patterned chiyogami paper for the third layer
- 1 sheet of 3 x 7 cm patterned chiyogami paper for the skirt
- 4 x 20 mm strip of patterned chiyogami paper for the hair bow
- Scissors
- Clear glue

PATTERNS

- K1, K2, K3, K4, K5, Hair and Head templates (see page 158)

DIFFICULTY ✳✳

INSTRUCTIONS

1 Cut out 1 x hair and 1 x head templates using card paper and scissors. Glue the hair on to the face.

2 Cut a K3 template from card paper. Take the 9 x 9 cm sheet of patterned paper for the first layer.

3 Fold the paper in half and unfold.

4 Place the K3 template onto the back of the paper.

5 Fold the paper around the shape of the template.

6 Remove the template to leave the folded shape.

7 Take the two sheets of 3.5 x 7 cm paper and cut out 1 x K4 and 1 x K5 template using card paper.

8 Fold the paper around the shape of each template.

9 Remove the templates to leave the two opposite folded shapes for the second layer.

10 Take the two sheets of 6 x 12 cm paper and cut out 1 x K1 and 1 x K2 template using card paper.

11 Fold one of the pieces of paper in half and hold the card paper K1 template against the patterned side one of the paper strips, as shown.

12 Follow the template to cut away the bottom curve.

13 Fold the top corners over the the template.

14 Repeat steps 11–13 on the other piece of paper and K2 template.

15 Place the K2 piece on top of the K1 piece and fit together in the top corner point. Secure with glue.

16 Take the 3 x 7 cm piece of patterned paper for the skirt.

17 Pleat fold at either side of the paper to meet in the middle.

18 Flip over and fold both edges of the top layer to the middle.

19 Unfold the bottom layer.

20 Bring the left side in towards the middle pleat, folding along your mountain crease to create a layer on top. Repeat on the right side.

21 Bring the two middle pleats together at the top and crease to make a trapezoid skirt shape.

22 Take the tiny paper strip, fold it into a ring and use glue to fix it together.

23 Fold in half then cut out the shape of a bow.

24 To assemble, it is easiest to start with the top layer. First, glue the head behind the top tip of your joined pieces from step 15 (K1 and K2 templates). Then glue the two pieces from step 9 (K4 and K5 templates) onto the back of the top layer, leaving the desired amount of corners on the sides. Glue the skirt to the back of the second layer, making sure the pleats are showing at the front. Finally, attach the large piece from step 6 (K3 template) behind the skirt to hold the kimono together, and glue the bow to the hair.

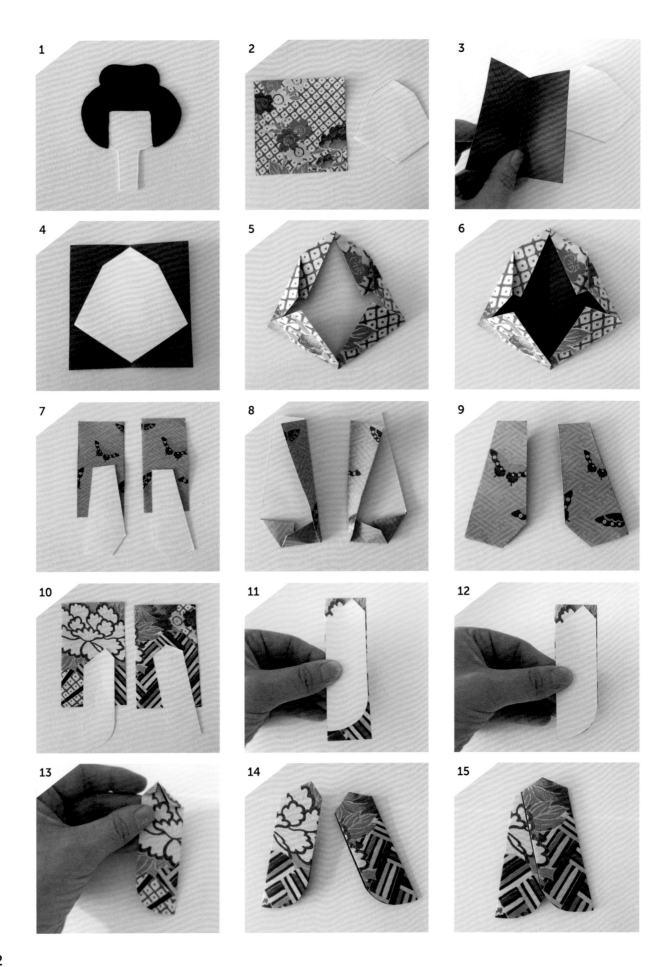

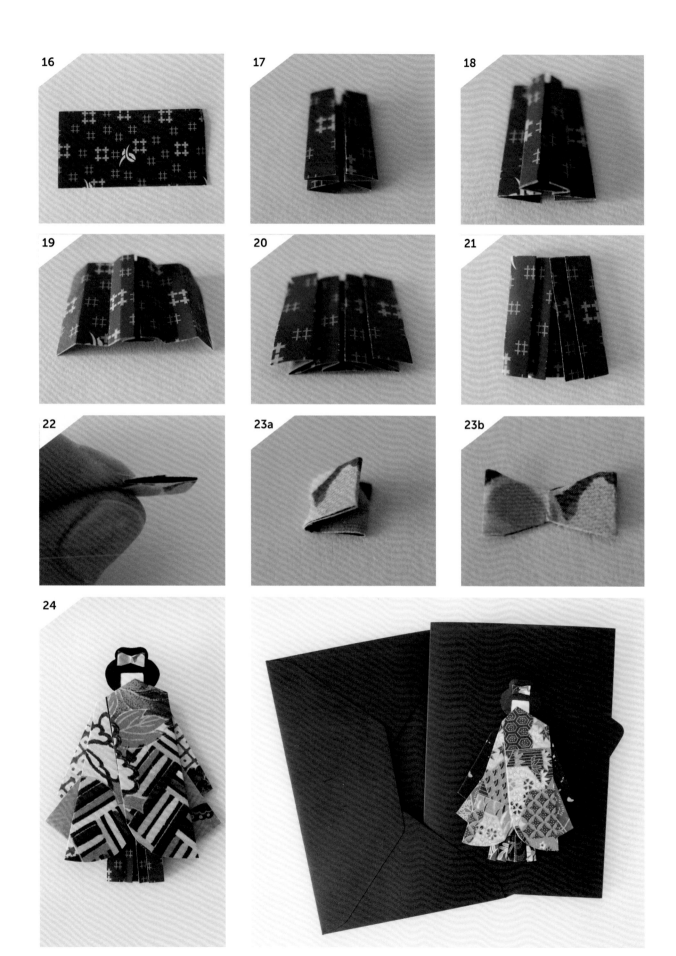

LET IT SNOW!

These snowflakes are perfect for a wintry greeting card, or make smaller ones and hang them with string to create a decorative flurry inside.

MATERIALS
- 2 sheets of 15 x 15 cm paper

DIFFICULTY ✳✳

INSTRUCTIONS

1 Fold across both diagonals and unfold.

2 Fold in half and unfold.

3 Fold the top and bottom edges to the centre line and unfold.

4 Turn 90 degrees anticlockwise. Fold in half and unfold.

5 Fold the top and bottom edges to the centre line and unfold. You will now have 16 squares.

6 Turn the paper over. Fold each corner to the centre point.

7 Turn the paper over. Follow the central mountain creases and bring the four sides (red dots) to the centre. Squash down the top flaps to create a square. It will look like this!

8 Turn the paper over. Fold the corners to the centre point.

9 Unfold each flap out from behind. Your paper will now be a square.

10 Turn the paper over. Lift up one corner from the centre, open the inner pockets and fold up to the outer edge. It should form a rectangle.

11 Repeat step 10 on the other three flaps. You should have an inner square now.

12 Turn the paper over. On the top-right square, fold the sides of the top flap to the corner's central line, then unfold.

13 Lift up the top flap and mountain fold along the crease you just made. Inside reverse fold the shaded side behind, then flatten the diamond shape.

14 Bring the sides of the top flap to the centre line.

15 Repeat steps 12–14 on the other three squares.

16 Turn the paper over. Fold the straight edges down, folding from one corner to the next.

17 Turn your paper over. One snowflake is complete! Follow steps 1–17 to make another.

18 Choose one of your snowflakes and, on each side, valley fold the four small points towards the centre.

19 On your other snowflake, fold out each of the four corners so that you have the square underneath.

20 Turn your first snowflake 90 degrees clockwise and place it onto the square, then bring back over the four corners on top so that you have 8 points in total. Your snowflake is now complete!

TIP
To make a greeting card, apply clear glue to the back of your snowflake and stick onto an A5 card!

Scan for a tutorial!

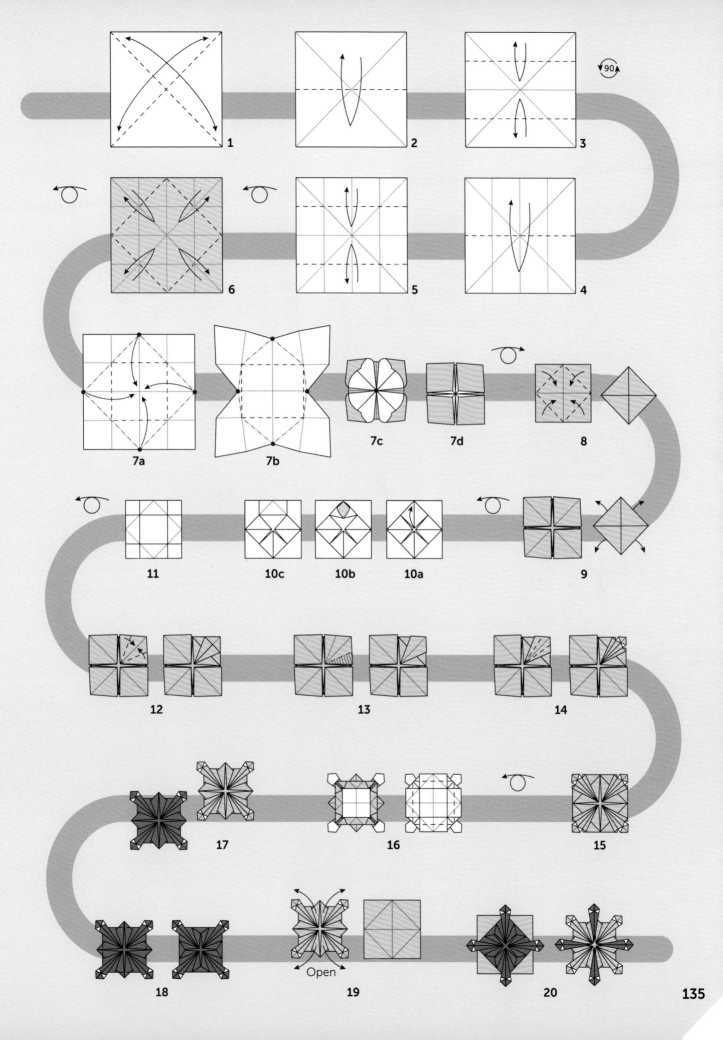

1

2

3

6

5

4

7a

7b

7c

7d

8

11

10c

10b

10a

9

12

13

14

17

16

15

18

19

20

SEASONAL DECORATIONS

Introduction

The joy of any holiday or celebration starts with the preparation, which always builds up a sense of anticipation and excitement. Although there are many celebration decorations available on the market, making them yourself will add a personal touch and can bring friends and family together to enjoy a fun and rewarding activity.

The paper that you choose for your decorations doesn't have to be high-quality or expensive. Coloured kraft paper, which comes in a roll up to 10 metres long and is available in many colours, is recommended as a cost-effective and easy-to-recycle material. Kraft paper is easy to fold and is great for large-scale decorations such as the Christmas Tree (see page 152). Metallic foil paper adds a superb shiny effect to the Festive Ornament (see page 150), while the Spooky Bat (see page 144) and Halloween Garland (see page 147) are simply made from 80 gsm black copy paper, which is readily available from stationery shops.

Get in the holiday spirit with the gorgeous origami Christmas Tree, which will sit in pride of place above the roaring fire on your mantlepiece. The unique Festive Ornament can be made in any shade to complement your Christmas colour scheme and looks great hung from the tree.

The Spooky Bat and Halloween Garland will add a chilling touch to any pre-trick-or-treat party, and these look so effective when hung together on the wall. Make as many as you can while listening to a spooky playlist or watching a scary movie for a whole lot of frightening fun!

You can transform those leftover scraps of paper that you can't bear to part with into gorgeous Paper Strip Decorations (see page 138–143). Find instructions over the next pages for how to make simple paper hearts, baubles and balls that can be combined with further strips or paper chains and hung from the ceiling to enhance the festivities.

PAPER STRIP DECORATIONS

All papercraft lovers have a box of precious scraps that just can't be thrown away. Now they can be transformed into beautiful decorations! The size of your paper scrap needn't matter; as long as you can cut a strip from it, you can use it.

MATERIALS

- Scrap paper (around 110 gsm or heavier strips of wrapping paper or similar is ideal)
- Cutter
- Cutting mat
- Ruler (optional)
- Double-sided tape or glue
- Wooden peg (to secure any glued parts while drying)

TIP

Use a metal ruler to easily cut all the strips to the same width (the width of the ruler). Without a ruler and cutting mat, you can just pleat fold the paper and cut.

DIFFICULTY ✶✶

HEARTS

These simple paper hearts make a sweet decoration
for a special anniversary or Valentine's Day.

INSTRUCTIONS

1 I used six paper strips in three colours: two 5 cm lengths, two 21 cm lengths and two 25 cm lengths, each with a width of 1.6 cm.

2 Glue or tape the two longest strips together at one end. The glued or taped area should be about a 1.6 cm square. I used a square of double-sided tape.

3 Attach the medium-length strips to the taped end, putting them either side of the long strips.

4 Stick the smallest length strips to the taped end, putting them either side of the medium-length strips.

5 Bring the unattached ends of both small strips up to the closed end, then glue or tape in place.

6 Repeat for the medium-length strips. You can adjust the shape by attaching the strips further down the end or a little before the end, but make sure both sides are attached at the same point to keep the shape symmetrical.

7 Repeat for the last two longest strips. The heart shape is complete!

1
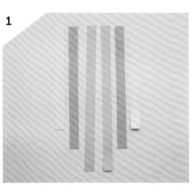

2a
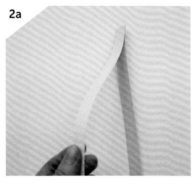

3a
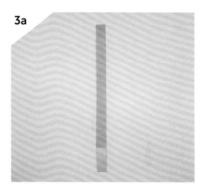

3b
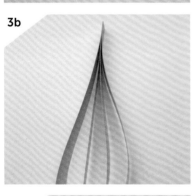

4a
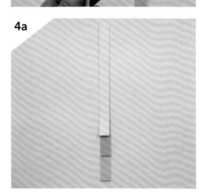

4b
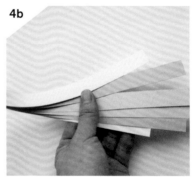

5
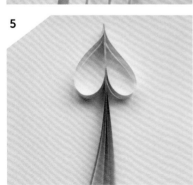

6
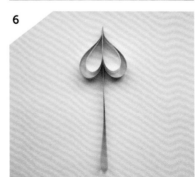

7
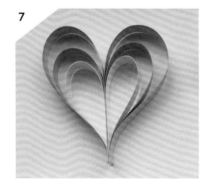

BAUBLES

These easy-to-make baubles can be made bigger simply by adding additional strips — just make sure each new strip layer is longer than the previous one.

INSTRUCTIONS

1 I used five paper strips in three colours: one 15 cm length, two 20 cm lengths and two 24 cm lengths, each with a width of 1.6 cm.

2 Attach all the paper strips at one end. Put the shortest one in the middle, the medium-length ones on both sides of it, then the longest ones on the outside.

3 Attach the medium-length strips to the other end of the short strip with tape or glue. Repeat with the longest strips on the outside.

4 Your bauble is now complete! Add more strips if desired.

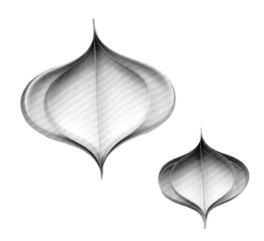

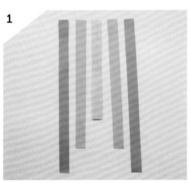
1

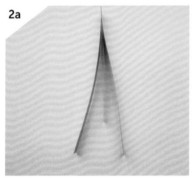
2a

2b

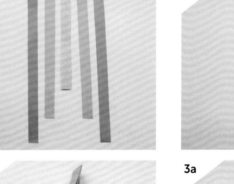
2c

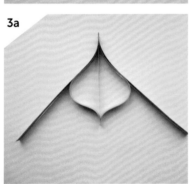
3a

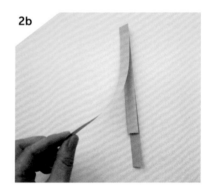
3b

4a

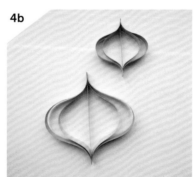
4b

BALLS

You won't believe how easy it is to make up these multicoloured paper balls from simple paper strip crosses.

INSTRUCTIONS

1 I used six paper strips, each of the same length, in three colours.

2 Attach two strips with tape or glue at the centre to make a cross.

3 Repeat to make two more crosses: one in each colour.

4 Attach the three crosses together at the centre. Keep an even space between the strips.

5 Bring two opposite ends from the same strip up and attach them together using glue or tape.

6 Repeat to bring the other two ends from this cross up and attach them together on top of the previous joint.

7 One by one, bring all the strips up in this way, attaching the ends at one point.

8 Your ball decoration is now complete!

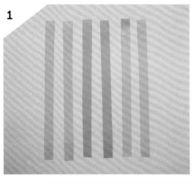

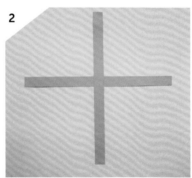

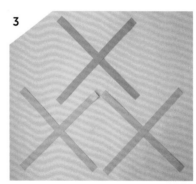

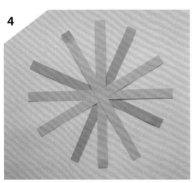

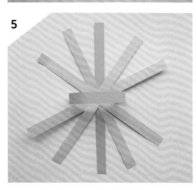

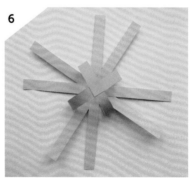

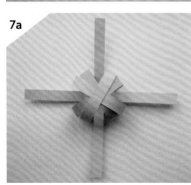

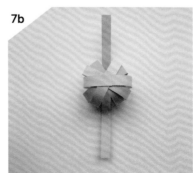

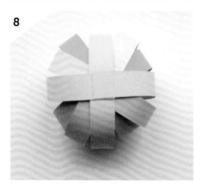

ASSEMBLING THE LINKS

Additional paper strips can be used to join together and hang your paper creations with pride. Enhance the look by making paper chains in complementary colours.

INSTRUCTIONS

Size Your adjoining paper strips can be any size – longer strips will give more of a gap between your decorations.

1 Apply tape or glue to one end of a paper strip and attach it to the top of your decoration.

2 Secure the other end of this paper strip to the bottom of your next ornament and continue adding as many as you desire to create a chain of decorations.

3 Alternatively, attach both ends of a strip to your decoration to form a ring. Make an interlinking ring by attaching the ends of the next strip together inside your first ring. Continue to create a paper chain of your desired length.

1a
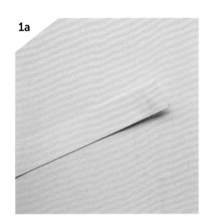

1b
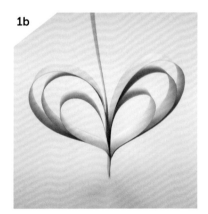

2
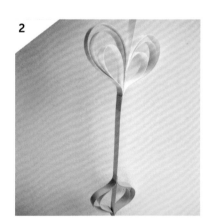

3a
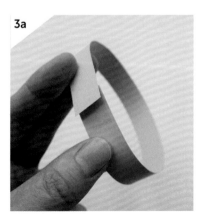

3b

3c
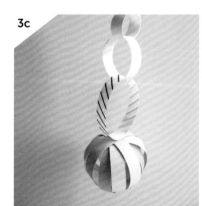

SPOOKY BAT

These bats make a chilling addition to any Halloween party, especially when hung in groups along with the Halloween Garland (see page 147).

MATERIALS
- 1 sheet of 21 x 21 cm black copy paper (or any size, as desired)

DIFFICULTY ✳✳✳

INSTRUCTIONS

1 Fold diagonally and unfold.

2 Fold diagonally from the other direction.

3 Fold the wide edge up by 1 cm.

4 Turn over and fold the other side.

5 Unfold completely.

6 Fold inwards at the second line, bringing the lower flap up on top.

7 Bring the remaining flap on top of the other, folding at the second line.

8 Unfold both flaps out.

9 This is what your paper should look like.

10 Turn over. Fold the pointed tip of one side inwards, then fold the top two corners in line with the edge of the paper behind.

11 Turn the paper over. Inside reverse fold on the top corner, then tuck in the fold.

12 Repeat step 11 on the other side.

13 Make a mountain fold along the middle horizontal line.

14 Bring the middle fold to where the lines cross over on its head.

15 Mountain fold to make the ears three dimensional.

16 Turn over. Follow the indicator lines to curve the neck and head. Pinch the ears.

17 Fold the tail up so it is level with the small flaps.

18 Bring the tail back down so it sticks out a little bit.

19 Fold the tail sides to the centre line to make it pointed.

20 Turn your paper over. Fold and unfold just off-centre of one wing.

21 Fold the tip of the wing to the folded line.

22 Fold the tip of the wing back onto itself.

23 Fold the whole wing over at your off-centre line.

24 Fold the outer edge inwards towards the body. Fold the wing back onto itself.

25 Unfold and spread out the wing.

26 Repeat steps 20–25 for the other wing.

27 Fold the top of the body underneath.

28 Use mountain folds to curve the wing's edges underneath.

29 Repeat for each section, and on the other wing.

30 Your Spooky Bat is now finished!

Scan for a tutorial!

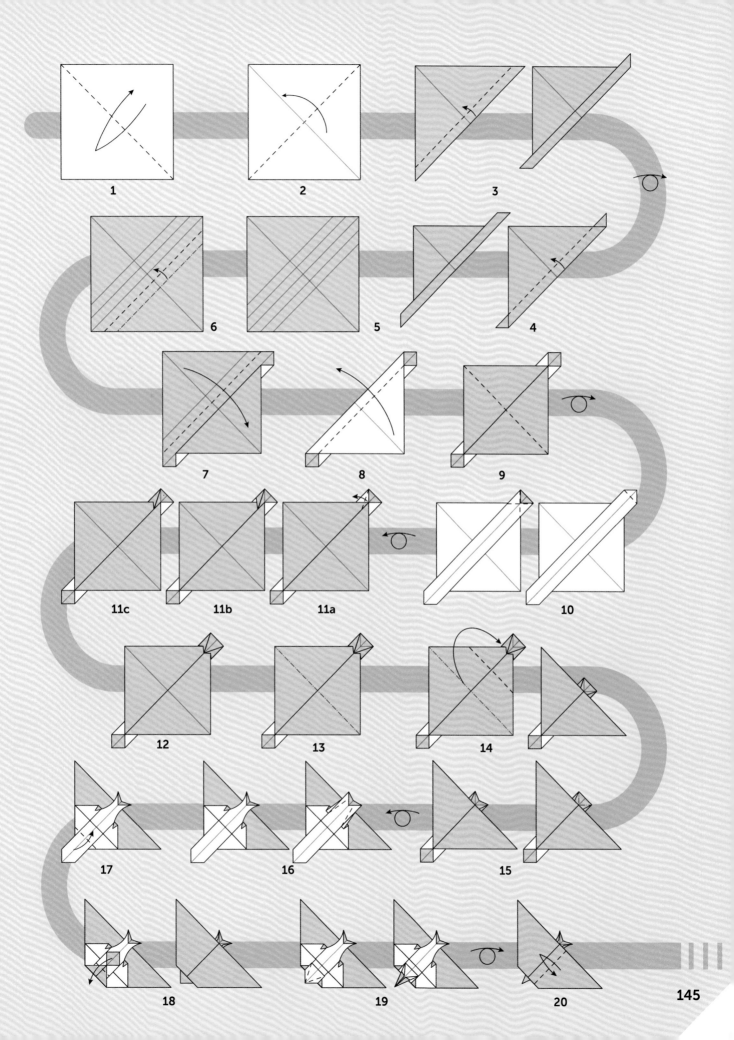

1

2

3

4

5

6

7

8

9

10

11a

11b

11c

12

13

14

15

16

17

18

19

20

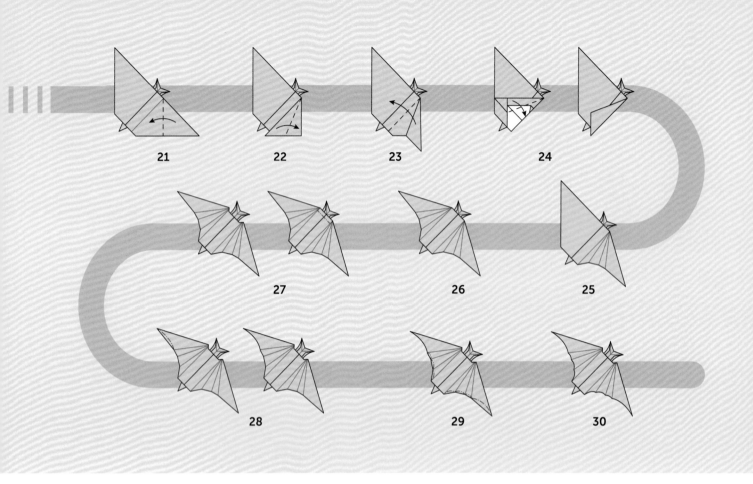

21 22 23 24

27 26 25

28 29 30

HALLOWEEN GARLAND

You can adapt the length of this spooky garland by using as many sheets of paper as you wish. The repetitive cutting out of each section is quite therapeutic.

MATERIALS

- Even number of sheets of 20 x 20 cm (or larger) black copy paper
- Scissors
- Clear glue

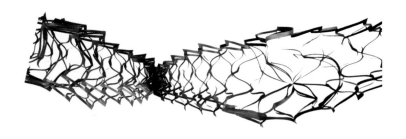

DIFFICULTY ✷✷

INSTRUCTIONS

1 Fold the paper in half.

2 Fold the top right corner down to the bottom edge, then unfold.

3 Fold the bottom right corner up to the top edge, then unfold.

4 Bring the top left corner across to where the diagonal lines cross.

5 Fold the left side back on itself.

6 Fold the right side down so that it lines up next to the left edge.

7 Mountain fold between the flaps to bring the right-hand side behind.

8 It should look like this.

9 Turn your paper 90 degrees anticlockwise. Cut off the paper above the top triangle flap.

10 Your paper should look like this.

11 Cut a line from the left edge to the right, leaving a small gap before the end, then repeat going right to left edge. Keep the cutting lines close and parallel to each other. Repeat all the way to the end.

12 Unfold the pentagon shape but be careful of the cut layers.

1	2	3
	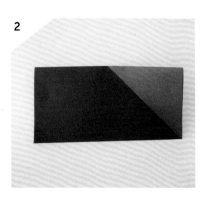	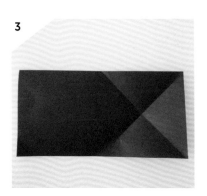

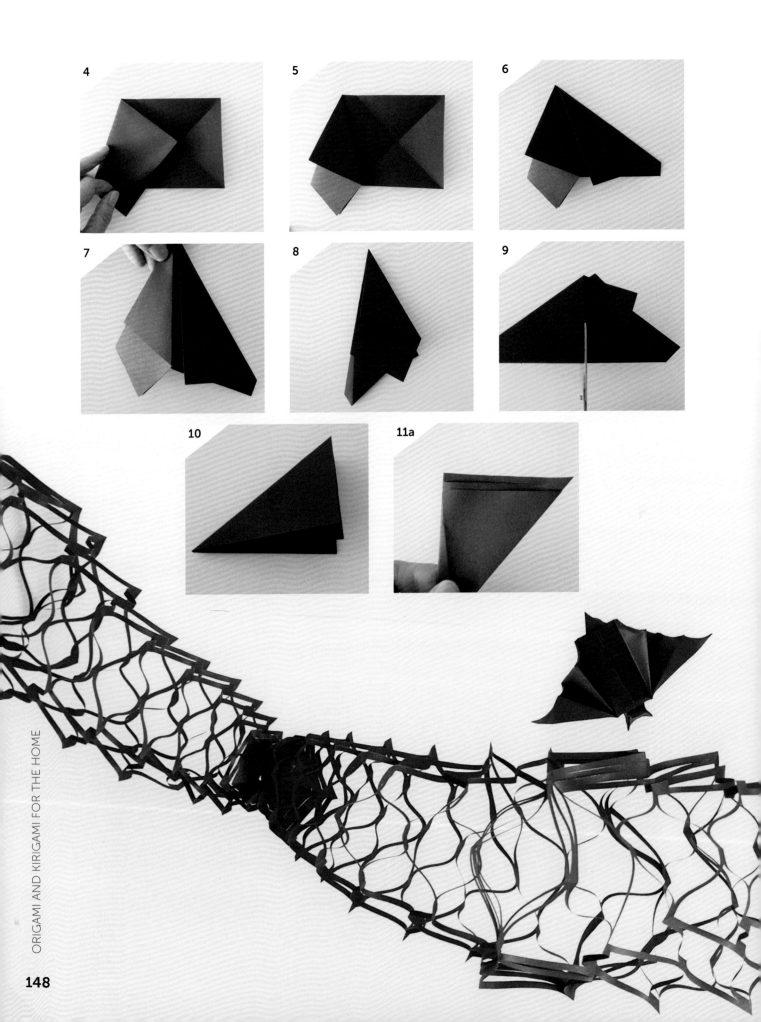

11b

12

13

14

15

16

13 Apply a small amount of glue to all five corners.

14 Repeat steps 1–13 to make another pentagon. Place one pentagon on top of the other and stick down the five glued corners.

15 Apply a small amount of glue to the centre of the top layer. Repeat

steps 1–13 to make another pentagon, then place on top, making sure only the centre is glued between the second and the third layers.

16 When the glue has dried out completely, stretch out your finished Halloween Garland.

Repeat steps 1–15, in groups of three pentagons, until you reach the desired length for your garland.

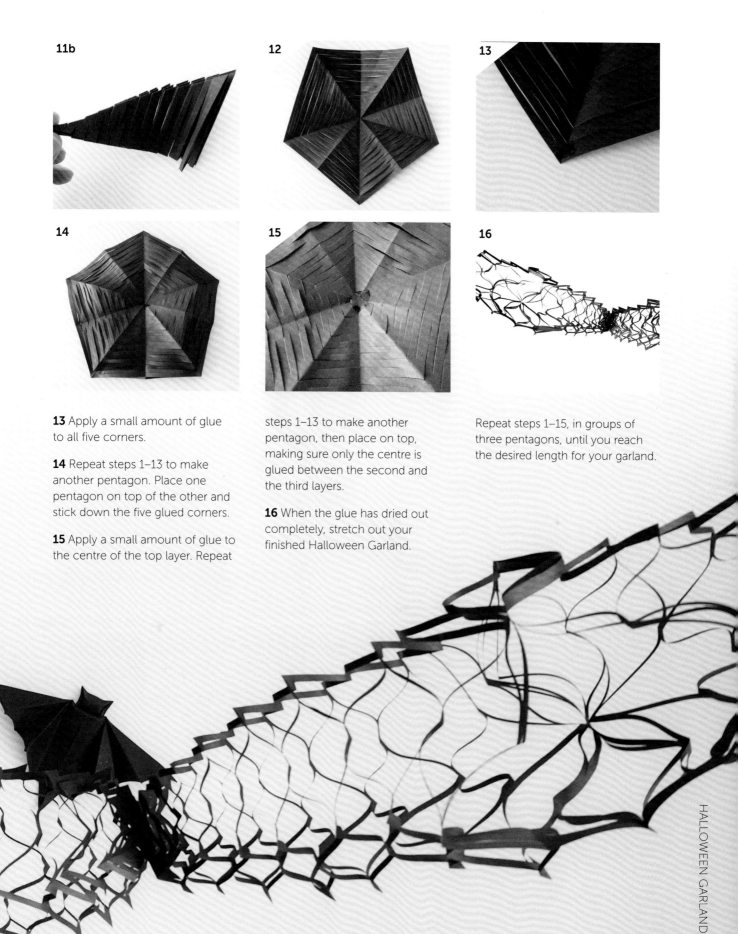

FESTIVE ORNAMENT

Why not add a little string or ribbon and hang this classic design from your Christmas tree?

MATERIALS

- 1 sheet of 15 x 15 cm metallic foil paper

DIFFICULTY ✳

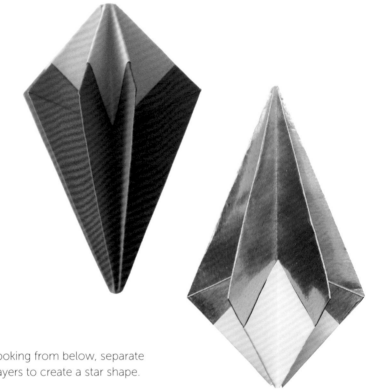

INSTRUCTIONS

1 Fold across both diagonals and unfold. Turn the paper over.

2 Flip over. horizontally and vertically, then unfold.

3 Follow the existing creases to make a waterbomb base.

4 Turn your paper so that one triangle is facing you, then squash fold the front triangle.

5 Fold the corner point up so that it lines up with the bottom edge.

6 Repeat steps 4–5 on the remaining flaps.

7 With one folded triangle facing you, bring the right-hand side over onto the left.

8 Fold the bottom left and right corners up to the centre line.

9 Repeat on the other sides. Your paper will look like this.

10 Looking from below, separate the layers to create a star shape.

11 Your Festive Ornament is now complete!

TIP
To hang, thread a needle with a thin thread or cotton and poke just under the ornament's top point. Tie in a loop and hang on your tree!

Scan for a tutorial!

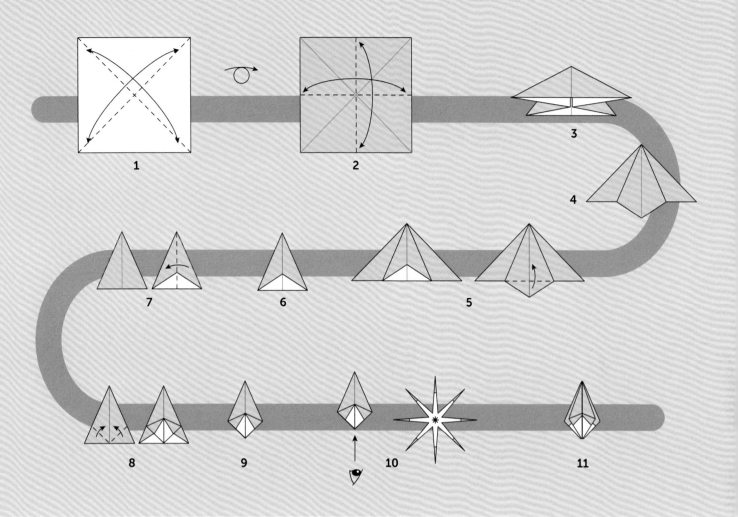

CHRISTMAS TREE

These three-dimensional paper Christmas trees make beautiful decorations to adorn your mantlepiece over the festive season.

MATERIALS

- 3 sheets of green paper for the branches: 20 x 20 cm, 17.5 x 17.5 cm, 15 x 15 cm
- 1 sheet of 15 x 15 cm brown paper for the trunk
- Tacky or clear glue

DIFFICULTY ✱✱✱

INSTRUCTIONS

Branches

1 Fold across both diagonals and unfold.

2 Fold in half and unfold.

3 Fold the top and bottom edges to the centre line and unfold.

4 Turn 90 degrees anticlockwise. Fold in half and unfold.

5 Fold the top and bottom edges to the centre line and unfold.

6 Turn the paper over. Fold each corner to the centre point.

7 Turn the paper over. Fold each corner to the first fold line.

8 Follow the central mountain creases and bring the four sides (red dots) to the centre. Squash down the top flaps to create a square with an inner diamond.

9 On the bottom right corner, fold over the left side of one corner flap on top of the right side, and unfold.

10 Lift open the left-hand flap and bring the outer left edge to the corner's centre line.

11 Valley fold and flatten the paper on top of the folded left flap so that the central line is back in its original position.

12 Repeat steps 9–11 on all the remaining flaps.

13 Turn the paper over. Mountain fold along the left centre crease line, and bring the paper up to the upper diagonal crease line.

14 Fold the top corner of the folded paper down.

15 Repeat steps 13–14 on the other three crease lines. This will raise the other side to a point.

16 Turn the paper over. Looking at one of your flaps, tuck the left side into the shaded pocket behind.

17 Mountain fold the right-hand flap and tuck into the flap behind. The two folded triangles will be facing outwards now. Repeat steps 16–17 and tuck in on each triangle.

18 Turn your paper so that the point faces you. Mountain fold the right flap of the raised triangles and tuck it behind, then repeat for all the remaining triangles. You will now have smaller leaves.

19 One set of branches is complete. Repeat steps 1–18 to make two more using the smaller-sized papers.

Scan for a tutorial!

ORIGAMI AND KIRIGAMI FOR THE HOME

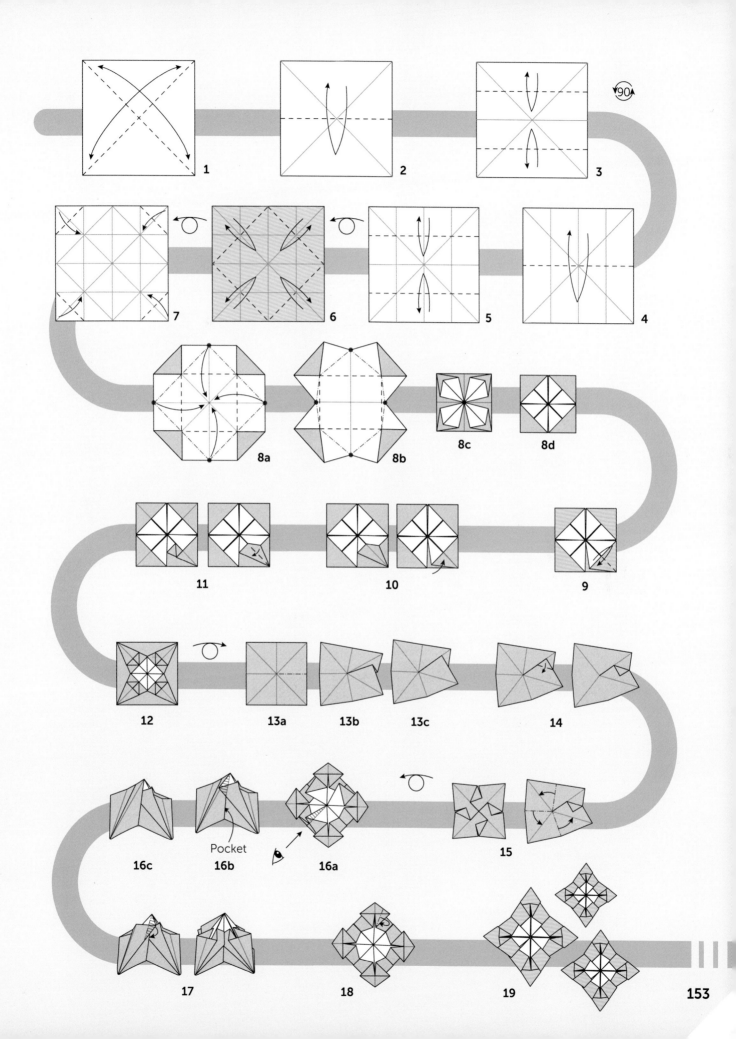

Trunk

1 Fold across both diagonals and unfold.

2 Flip over. Fold in half horizontally and vertically, then unfold.

3 Turn over and rotate 90 degrees anticlockwise. Follow the mountain fold creases to form a square base. The bottom point will be open.

4 Bring the left flap over the centre line and squash fold.

5 Repeat on all flaps.

6 Fold the left and right corners to the centre line and unfold.

7 Lift the top layer up and bring both sides to the middle, along the crease lines. Flatten the diamond shape.

8 Fold down the tip of the diamond to the centre line. Repeat steps 7–8 on the other three sides.

9 Turn 180 degrees. Pull apart the end flaps, then follow the top triangle crease on one diamond shape and mountain fold to tuck it inside.

10 Repeat step 9 on all the flaps, and then bring together again.

11 Fold the left and right corners of the top layer to the centre line. Repeat on the other sides.

12 Separate apart again and bring forward the creased flaps. Flatten each, then fold down the pointed tip. Repeat for each flap.

13 Untuck the shaded flap and push into the middle to shape the sides and make four slightly separate segments of the trunk. Repeat for each side.

14 Turn 180 degrees. The trunk is complete!

15 Layer up the branches onto the trunk, starting with the largest and topping with the smallest and gluing them in place. Your Christmas Tree is now finished!

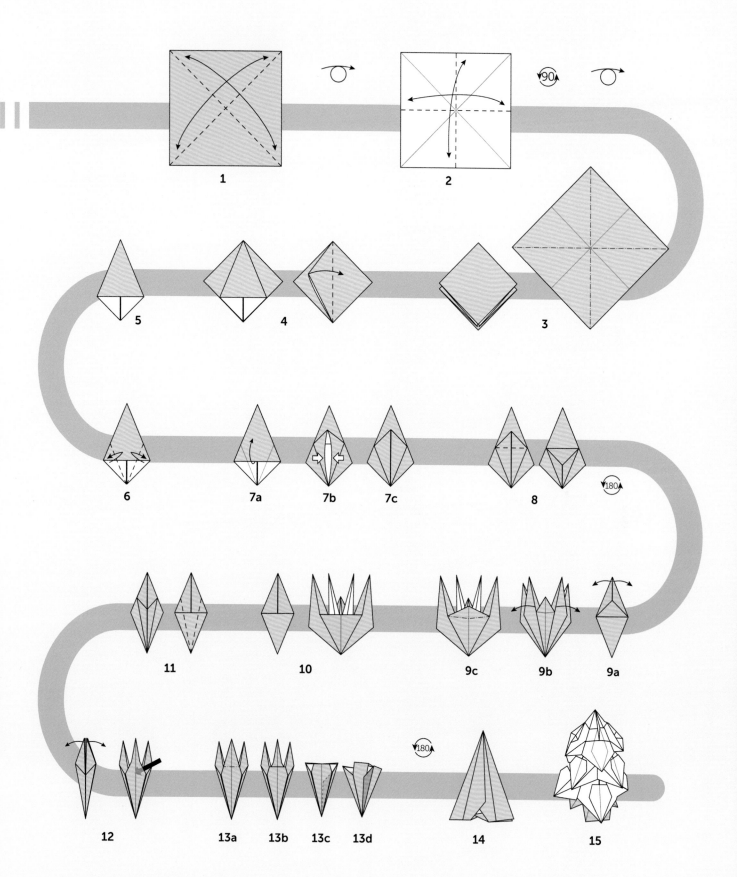

1

2

3

4

5

6

7a

7b

7c

8

9a

9b

9c

10

11

12

13a

13b

13c

13d

14

15

PATTERNS

Rose Wall Panel (page 62) and Romantic Rose (page 91)

Petals

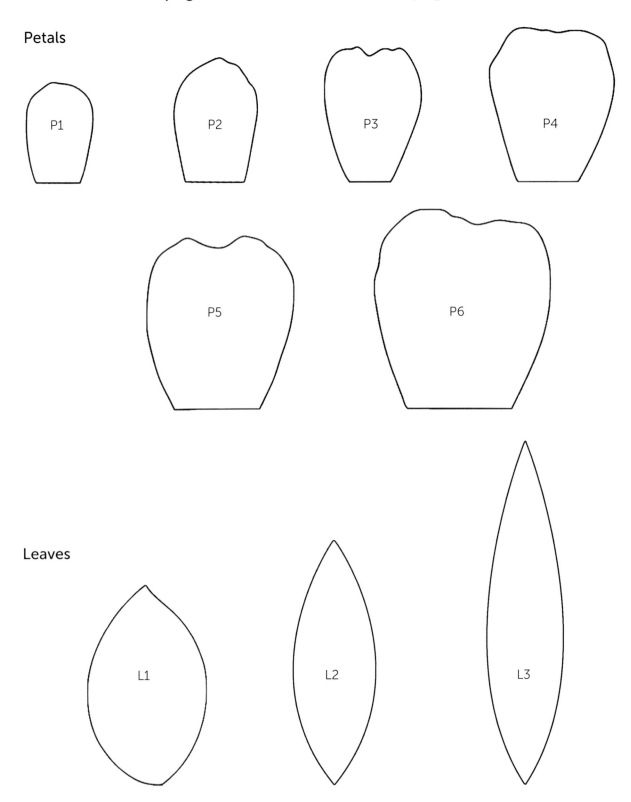

P1

P2

P3

P4

P5

P6

Leaves

L1

L2

L3

Brilliant Butterflies (page 65)

Feathered Crane (page 84), Sandhill Crane (page 86), Exotic Crane (page 88), Tant Crane (page 90)

Type A Feathers

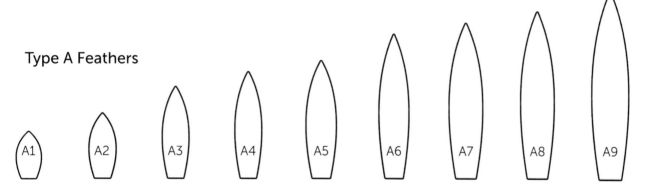

Type B Feathers

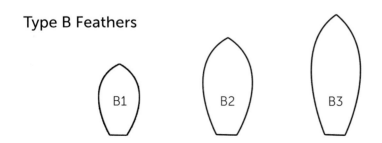

Paper Doll in Kimono (page 130)

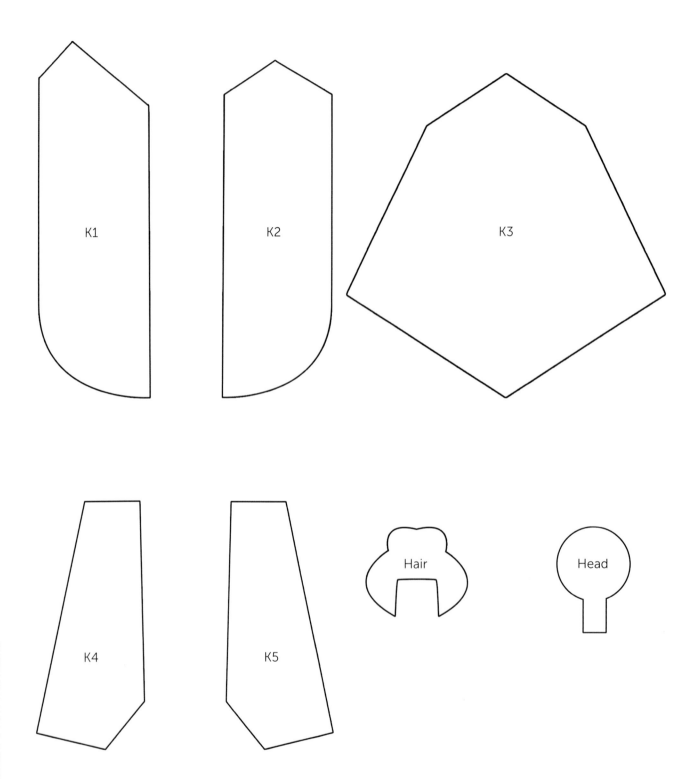

K1

K2

K3

K4

K5

Hair

Head

ABOUT THE AUTHOR

I first got into origami and papercrafting eight years ago, while working in my paper art shop. To promote the paper being sold, I began making origami butterflies to display around the shop. I then went on to making papier mâché and kirigami displays for the shop window. During this time, I discovered origami bucky ball, which was when my passion for origami really grew. As someone with a scientific background, geometric origami is the area that interests me most.

The Five Intersecting Tetrahedra by Thomas Hull is what got me interested in the maths behind origami. Learning how to piece it together and read the folded paper inspired me to teach origami to others. From then, I began teaching origami workshops, which soon moved on to wider business events and parties.

Creating bespoke decorations for restaurants and shops has continuously improved my papercrafting skills. I have spent a lot of time learning how different paper types and printing techniques give different results, which in turn give me the best options for my origami projects and the ability to advise customers on materials.

I love the challenge of complex origami models alongside easier papercrafts. Most of my origami designs stem from simple geometric forms, which I like to make with a group of friends while enjoying afternoon tea.

The instructions I give in this book can be used as an introduction to papercraft. Once you understand the concept behind the folds and structures, there are no strict rules in following the step-by-step instructions – they can be adapted to make your models unique to you.